I0539165

WARFARE
AND
DELIVERANCE

What Darkness Hopes You Never See

BREAK FREE ~ STAY FREE

FOUNDATIONAL TOOLS FOR
WARFARE & DELIVERANCE

WARFARE N DELIVERANCE

What Darkness Hopes You Never See

BREAK FREE ~ STAY FREE

TANYA D. NORWOOD

WARFARE AND DELIVERANCE
Break Free ~ Stay Free
What Darkness Hopes You Never See

Copyright © 2025 | by Tanya D. Norwood | All Rights Reserved

TDScript Publishing

ISBN 979-8-218-78494-2

No part of this publication may be reproduced, stored in a retrieval system or transmitted in any way by means, electronic, mechanical, photocopy, recording or otherwise without the prior permission of the author except as provided by USA copyright law.

Scripture quotations marked (KJV) and those not marked are taken from the King James Version of *The Holy Bible*.

Scripture quotations marked (NLT) are taken from *The Holy Bible, New Living Translation*, copyright © 1996, 2004, 2015 by Tyndale House Foundation. Used by permission of Tyndale House Publishers, Inc., Carol Stream, Illinois 60188. All rights reserved.

Scriptures marked (NKJV) are taken from the *New King James Version*, copyright © 1982 by Thomas Nelson. Used by permission. All rights reserved.

Scriptures marked (AMP) are taken from the *Amplified Bible*, copyright © 2015 by The Lockman Foundation La Habra, California 90631. Used by permission. All rights reserved.

The opinions expressed by the author are those of Tanya D. Norwood

TABLE OF CONTENTS

DEDICATION

To God—the Father, the Son, and the Holy Spirit—Your salvation, love, grace, and mercy are the very foundation of my life and the reason I live with purpose. Thank You for loving me unconditionally, healing the broken places, and using my journey as a testimony of Your faithfulness. Every step I've taken and every word of encouragement I give is because of You. With a grateful heart, I give You all the Glory, Honor, and Praise, now and forever.

FROM THE AUTHOR

Dear Reader,

This book highlights my journey of what it looks like to be in the middle of a battle and not know how to fight. I wanted to share what it looks like to be saved, in love with Jesus, but still experiencing spiritual struggles. How can a person be saved, yet feel bound, weary, or stuck?

What I didn't realize at the time was that I had stepped into something very real: spiritual warfare. The kind that doesn't just touch the surface of your life—it targets your mind, your identity, your purpose, and your very relationship with God. The enemy was relentless in trying to keep me discouraged, defeated, and disconnected from the freedom that Jesus died to give me.

When I first came to the Lord, I did not understand the authority we have in Christ. I knew of His love, but I knew nothing about fighting battles. Looking back, I now see how tenderly and faithfully God covered me in those early years. As I grew in faith, I realized I wasn't meant to stay in hiding or live in defeat. The correct response was to fight.

To be completely honest, I didn't want to fight. I wanted comfort. I wanted safety. If I could paint the picture for you, it would be me clinging to God with all my strength, trying to stay behind. But The Lord kept gently nudging me onto the battlefield anyway. When I finally surrendered, He began to train me—spiritually, emotionally, and mentally. He taught me about spiritual authority—what it truly means to walk in my identity as a child of God. He opened my eyes to the power of deliverance, the beauty of healing, and the unshakable truth that makes us free.

This book is the fruit of that journey. It's filled with lessons I've learned, moments of raw honesty, and scriptural truths that have brought real lasting change to my life. I don't believe my story is unique. Many in the Body of Christ know what it is like to be saved yet still struggling. Or to be passionate about God but quietly fighting battles that no one sees.

If this sounds like you, this book was written with you in mind.

With love,
Tanya

INTRODUCTION

When you hear the term *spiritual warfare*, what comes to mind? Maybe intense scenes from a movie, casting out demons, breaking curses, or battling unseen forces. And while that's part of it, spiritual warfare is so much more than dramatic encounters. It's something that affects our everyday lives in ways we may not realize.

Before stepping into any battle, especially a spiritual one, we need to be grounded. Think of it as building a house, without a strong foundation the structure can't stand. And with weak foundations instability occurs, making everything built on top—vulnerable to collapse. The same goes for our spiritual lives. If we don't have the right tools and understanding, we're left vulnerable. And this battle is not only about us, but it also impacts our families, relationships, purpose, and even the legacy we leave behind.

Here's the thing: whether we acknowledge it or not, we're in the middle of a fight. Ignoring it doesn't make it go away. The only real choice we have is whether we'll prepare for it or not.

One of the key aspects of spiritual warfare is *deliverance*. This topic gets a lot of attention. People have many opinions about it, and sometimes, it can even create division within the church. But that's not what this conversation is about. Instead, let's look at what Scripture says. What is deliverance? Who is it for? And how do we walk in it? These are the questions we'll unpack together. Building on truth, not trends, and seeking understanding that stands firm, no matter the battle.

SECTION I:
THE FOUNDATION

WARFARE AND DELIVERANCE

TANYA D. NORWOOD

CHAPTER 1:
WHAT IS DELIVERANCE?

Simply put, deliverance means to be set free. In the Old Testament, deliverance often meant freedom from physical enemies such as oppressors, invading armies, or captors—and one of the most powerful examples of this is seen in the life of Moses.

In Exodus 2:23 and 3:7-10, we see that God heard the cries of His people in bondage. They were enslaved in Egypt, crushed under the weight of oppression. But God didn't stay silent. At the appointed time God chose Moses to go to Pharaoh and declare, "Let My people go." It was a command, and it was a declaration of their freedom. God wasn't just pulling them out of slavery; He was calling His people into purpose. He wanted them to walk in liberty, to worship Him freely, and to live as His chosen people—not bound, but blessed.

Fast forward to the New Testament, and the mission of deliverance is still front and center. But something is different. Now we get a behind the scenes perspective of what it looks like to fight spiritually. We know what a physical fight looks like, but now we see Jesus opposing the spiritual ones. Jesus directly addressed the demons of torment, and oppression. And Jesus had the authority to cast them out. He healed, delivered, and restored.

In addition to salvation, deliverance was not a side note in Jesus' ministry; it was one of the core expressions of His love. Jesus came to destroy the works of the devil (1 John 3:8), and that included setting people free from everything that held them captive, body, soul, and spirit. So, whether it was Pharaoh in Egypt or a demonic stronghold in a person's life, the message was the same: Deliverance.

In Mark chapter 1, a lot happens as Jesus launches His public ministry. He's baptized by John the Baptist, overcomes temptation in the wilderness, and begins calling His first disciples. But what is eye catching is that we're also introduced to Jesus' first recorded deliverance. Starting in verse 21, Jesus enters the synagogue on the Sabbath and begins teaching. But he doesn't teach like the Jewish leaders. The people immediately notice something different. Jesus spoke with authority.

Now imagine this: you're sitting in a worship service, and suddenly someone in the congregation yells out—Leave us alone! What have we to do with You, Jesus of Nazareth? Have You come to destroy us? I know who You are—the Holy One of God. That is what happened. A man in the synagogue possessed by an unclean spirit recognized Jesus' divinity and reacted in fear. Jesus simply rebukes the spirit and commands it to leave the man—and it does. Seeing this was not only powerful, but it was unlike anything the people had ever seen. Verse 27 captures their amazement:

> *"And they were all amazed, insomuch that they questioned among themselves, saying, What thing is this? what new doctrine is this? for with authority commandeth he even the unclean spirits, and they do obey him."*
>
> –Mark 1:27 KJV

In the Old Testament, people understood the reality of evil spirits and could recognize when someone was afflicted or possessed by them. This same knowledge was known in the New Testament. However, in the New Testament, when Jesus cast out demons with undeniable authority, the people were stunned because they had never seen such power over them. Jesus wasn't just walking around talking about the Kingdom; He was demonstrating it.

One Scripture that transformed my understanding of Kingdom demonstration is Luke 11:20 KJV, Jesus says, *"But if I with the finger of God cast out devils, no doubt the Kingdom of God is come upon you."* So, when demons are cast out, it's a display of Jesus' authority. It's His undeniable evidence that the Kingdom of God is here and at work. Matthew 6:10 KJV says: "Thy Kingdom come. Thy will be done in earth, as it is in heaven". Deliverance isn't just a spiritual encounter, it's a manifestation of God's will on earth destroying the works of the devil.

Some people believe deliverance and casting out demons were only meant for the early church, and they no longer need to be practiced. Jesus' words suggest otherwise. In Luke 11:24 KJV, Jesus reveals that when an evil spirit is cast out, it doesn't simply disappear. The passage says, *"When the unclean spirit is gone out of a man, he walketh through dry places, seeking rest; and finding none, he saith, I will return unto my house whence I came out."*

When the evil spirit returns to the old "house" (the person), verse 25 says the unclean spirit finds the house swept clean and in order. So in effort to cause confusion to order, the evil spirit brings backup. Verse 26 says that it brings seven spirits more wicked than itself. Then they all enter into the person and dwell there. This tells us two things. Evil spirits are still active after being cast out, and they are actively looking for another place to inhabit.

We see this cluster of demonic activity vividly in Mark chapter 5, where Jesus cast out a legion of demons from a single man. A legion is thousands. This can be hard to comprehend. How is that possible—how can one person be tormented by so many demons? But over time, I learned that demons often work in groups. They're organized, but like a gang.

In deliverance, the lead demon is often referred to as the strongman, the dominant spirit calling the shots. The others are called routing demons—spirits that tag along and reinforce the strongman's influence. For example, if the strongman is the *spirit of offense*, the routing demons might be unforgiveness, bitterness, anger, wrath, hatred, jealousy, and even murder. That's a gang of eight already. And often, these "gangs" continue to link up with other evil spirits—multiplying the spiritual oppression in a person's life.

The word "rout" has a few meanings, but from a spiritual perspective, it describes how demons "rout" or aggressively overtake and destabilize a person's life. These spirits try to invade, confuse, and conquer every area of a person's soul until they're spiritually overwhelmed.

When you begin to see deliverance as something vital, Biblical, and Kingdom-centered, your perspective changes and you begin to understand why it was an important part of Jesus' ministry. In the Kingdom of God, freedom is an unmistakable sign of Jesus' presence. Where He is, chains break, burdens lift, and souls are set free.

In Matthew 8:28, there were two men possessed by demons who came out from the tombs, wild and violent. Their presence was so fierce that no one dared to pass through that area; they had become a territorial stronghold. But when they saw Jesus, everything changed. The demons immediately recognized the Lord. Knowing that they had no choice but to leave, they asked the Lord if they were about to be tormented before their appointed time. Panicked, the demons asked Jesus to send them into a nearby herd of pigs. Jesus gave them a single command: **"Go."** And in that moment, thousands of demons fled, completely powerless in resisting His authority.

Can you imagine that entire herd suddenly filled with the torment of those unclean spirits? The pigs rushed violently down a steep *hillside* and drowned in the water. I would imagine that they were overwhelmed by the spiritual forces that were inside of them, but here is the point I want to make. The pigs drowned, but the demons didn't. They're still roaming around seeking bodies to inhabit, minds to torment, lives to manipulate, and souls to destroy. So when we ask, "is deliverance for today?", the answer is clear. Absolutely!

Mark chapter 5 and Luke chapter 8 are parallel accounts of this event in Matthew. I would encourage you to read all 3 of the disciple's review of this event. However, I want to share further details that are recorded in the gospel of Mark and Luke. After the demons were cast out into the pigs, the news about what happened spread fast. Soon after the people in that city saw a man sitting at the feet of Jesus, *clothed and in his right mind.* He was no longer mentally and spiritually oppressed.

He was no longer naked nor was he bound by mental and physical afflictions. Now he was clothed, and his shame, vulnerability and brokenness were removed. He had mental clarity, peace, and emotional stability. These visible changes were *undeniable signs* of his deliverance. Grateful, he wanted to go with Jesus, but the Lord told him to return to his home and show them the great things God had done for him. He was a walking testimony of the goodness of God.

With all of these scriptures, we can see that deliverance is still needed. At some point throughout our lifetime, we will encounter someone who is burdened by demonic oppression. Jesus didn't just minister deliverance. Through the power and authority of His Name, Jesus has equipped the Church to do the same. Deliverance is not outdated; it remains a vital part of ministry today.

SELF-REFLECTION QUESTIONS

1. Have I unknowingly avoided or dismissed the ministry of deliverance?

2. What steps can I take to learn more about deliverance?

CHAPTER 2:
WHAT I LEARNED FROM MARK CHAPTER 16

One day, as I was reading Mark chapter 16, I decided to read it in a few different Bible translations. I wanted to see how other versions phrased it. As I began looking at other translations, a notation caught my eye. It reads: *"The most ancient manuscripts of Mark conclude with verse 16:8."*

Wait... what? Were they saying that out of 19 verses in Mark 16, the last 10 were eliminated? I was surprised and unsettled. If those verses had been left out of the earlier manuscripts, that would run the risk of changing the entire context of the chapter. And why would someone want to do that? Why would someone want to remove them? The more I thought about it, the more it bothered me. Knowing that earlier manuscripts excluded the last 10 verses made me want to dig deeper and closely read everything after verse eight.

Verse 9 says, *"Now when Jesus was risen early the first day of the week, he appeared first to Mary Magdalene, out of whom he had cast seven devils."* My first thought was, of course, the enemy wouldn't want this verse to be known. This testimony of Mary's deliverance from seven devils is not something the kingdom of darkness would want to see published.

Bothered by the fact that someone would purposely leave verse 9 out, I turned to the other Gospels to cross-reference the account. And sure enough, Luke also confirms that Mary Magdalene had been delivered from seven demons. So if verse 9 was removed from earlier translations, thankfully the truth was echoed elsewhere in scripture.

I could have stopped at verse 9 and not read any further, but I wanted to know every word after verse 8 for my own knowledge. What If someone tried to remove these scriptures in the future? I had to look at these verses closely. That way, if they were removed in the future, I would have already retained these scriptures in my heart. I continued to read.

Verses 10 through 14 details Jesus's appearance to others after His resurrection. But repeatedly when witnesses testified that Jesus was alive—no one believed them. In fact Jesus rebuked His disciples for their *stubborn unbelief* because they refused to believe the eyewitness accounts of His resurrection. I thought this was interesting because normally we only think about

CHAPTER 2: WHAT I LEARNED FROM MARK CHAPTER 16

doubting Thomas (John 20:29), as if he was the only one that did not believe. But as it relates to maintaining the integrity of the scriptures, thankfully the truth about the Lord's resurrection can be found in other books of the Bible. I continued to read.

Verses 15 and 16 talk about the Great Commission, which is also found in Matthew 28:19–20. And Jesus also proceeds to tell His disciples that those who believe and are baptized will be saved and those that refuse to believe will be condemned. A message of warning that can again be found in other books.

And then I came to verse 17, which also happens to be one of my favorite scriptures. However, on that day, I had a new perspective on this verse. Verse 17 says, "And these signs shall follow them that believe; In my name shall they cast out devils;". That's when I stopped. Two things got my attention with this verse for the first time. Something I hadn't thought about before. First, verses 10 through 16 walks us through what unbelief looks like, then the first part of verse 17 tells us what happens when we believe. Secondly, The Lord is giving us a "list" of signs. And the first sign on the list "begins" with cast out devils. Just as verse 9 starts off by saying Mary was delivered from seven demons, the first sign on the list was cast out devils.

Allow me to pause for a moment to explain why this hit me the way that it did. To grasp why in those moments that verse caught my attention, we need to step back and remember something foundational. The Bible is not merely a book written by men, it was written by men *moved* by the Spirit of God. Yes, human hands penned the words, but all scriptures are God breathed (2 Timothy 3:16 AMP). Every word, every phrase, every order is strategically inspired, placed with purpose.

So when I read that Jesus began the list with, *"In my name shall they cast out devils;"* for me, that wasn't just a random starting point. That was intentional. I'm not saying the other signs are any less powerful. Each one plays a very important equal part in displaying what is obtained through the Lord's authority.

However, what I am saying is, the enemy doesn't want believers to grab hold of this promise. And I am sure that it was the enemy behind the idea of trying to have the verses removed. Satan knows that if every believer grabbed a hold of this promise to cast out devils, believers across the earth, generation after generation, would rise up in this truth, and hell itself would be shaken to its core.

Thankfully we have these Scriptures in the various translations today, but how often do we see people skip the first item on the list? The Scripture says these signs follow those who believe. Is it that we don't believe?

This is available to all Christians. We catch a glimpse of this in Mark chapter 9, when John told Jesus that they saw someone casting out devils in His Name. John stated that when they saw this, they stopped him because the man wasn't part of their group. Jesus corrected him. He made it clear that if the man was performing miracles in His Name, he was not against them, but for them (Mark 9:39-40). Jesus wasn't just endorsing the man's actions. By telling John not to stop the man casting out demons in His name, I believe Jesus was revealing that Kingdom connection is not determined by the proximity to the 12 disciples or group affiliations, but by aligning with God's purposes.

In John 10:16 (NLT), Jesus states, *"I have other sheep, too, that are not in this sheepfold."* In other words, the Kingdom isn't confined to one group of people. It's a global army of believers. Imagine what life would look like if we all lived this way—if every follower of Christ confidently walked in their God-given authority. We wouldn't be divided by affiliations, but united in purpose. Think of how much ground we could reclaim—for our families, our communities, and the world."

And let's not forget—those words in Mark chapter 16 are in red. They are straight from the mouth of Jesus. He's not just telling us what's possible, He's declaring what should be normal for the believer.

I remember early in my Christian walk, people would say, *"One of the devil's greatest tricks is convincing people he doesn't exist."* While that's still true, if I could rewrite that statement for today, I'd say this: One of the enemy's biggest tricks now is convincing believers that casting out devils is irrelevant for today, too radical to be true, or only for a select few. And as with any lie, those lies disarm people of the truth.

So for context, let's read the last 3 verses recorded in the book of Mark: " And these signs shall follow them that believe; In my name shall they cast out devils; they shall speak with new tongues; they shall take up serpents; and if they drink any deadly thing, it shall not hurt them; they shall lay hands on the sick, and they shall recover. So then after the Lord had spoken unto them, he was received up into heaven, and sat on the right hand of God. And they went forth, and preached every where, the Lord working with them, and confirming the word with signs following. Amen." (*Mark 16:17-20 KJV*).

SELF-REFLECTION QUESTIONS

1. Do I truly believe that I can walk in the power and authority that Jesus has granted me in His Name?

2. Am I living my life with faith and boldness, expecting the signs that Jesus spoke of to be evident in my life?

SECTION II:
THE CHRISTIAN DEBATE

WARFARE AND DELIVERANCE

TANYA D. NORWOOD

CHAPTER 3:
DO CHRISTIANS NEED DELIVERANCE?

One question that comes up time and time again is this: *"Do Christians need deliverance?"* It's a valid question—one that often sparks a lot of discussion and sometimes a heated debate. People go back and forth over the language. Are we talking about someone being possessed? Or is it oppression and influence? What do these terms mean, and how do we tell the difference?

Before we get tangled in definitions or theological arguments, let's take a step back and look at something Jesus said. Let's go straight to the Word! Let's look at Luke chapter 13 and let Scripture speak for itself.

> *And, behold, there was a woman who had a spirit*
> *of infirmity eighteen years, and was bowed together,*
> *and could in no wise lift up herself. And when Jesus*

saw her, he called her to him, and said unto her,
Woman, thou art loosed from thine infirmity. And
he laid his hands on her: and immediately she was
made straight, and glorified God. And the ruler of the
synagogue answered with indignation, because that
Jesus had healed on the sabbath day, and said unto
the people, There are six days in which men ought to
work: in them therefore come and be healed, and not
on the sabbath day. The Lord then answered him, and
said, Thou hypocrite, doth not each one of you on the
sabbath loose his ox or his ass from the stall, and lead
him away to watering? And ought not this woman,
being a daughter of Abraham, whom Satan hath
bound, lo, these eighteen years, be loosed from this
bond on the sabbath day?

–LUKE 13:11-16 KJV

This passage in Luke chapter 13 reveals two powerful truths—insights that often get overlooked when we talk about deliverance. First, we're told that the woman was *bound by a spirit.* Her condition wasn't the result of old age, bad posture, or an accident. The cause was clear: a spirit of infirmity had gripped her body for 18 long years, robbing her of her freedom and ability to stand upright. This wasn't a medical issue; it was a spiritual one.

Second, Jesus made it clear that this woman belonged to God. How do we know? He called her a daughter. Not just any daughter, but a daughter of Abraham, which is a title of covenant, heritage, and identity.

Now, some might say, being a descendant of Abraham doesn't necessarily mean she was saved, and that's true. When the Pharisees claimed Abraham as their father, Jesus let them know that He knew they were the offspring of Abraham. However, because they were trying to kill Jesus, the Lord's words and message could not be found in their hearts. Instead, they were of their father, the devil (John 8:37-44). Jesus pointed out that their spiritual DNA was different.

Jesus never said that about the woman in Luke chapter 13. He didn't correct her identity. He confirmed it. He didn't disqualify her. He defended her. But notice, despite her spiritual identity, she was still under demonic oppression. This is a critical point we can't ignore. She was a daughter of the promise, but she was still bound. The spirit of infirmity didn't "possess" her body—it "oppressed" her body, limiting her, crippling her, preventing her from living freely.

Oppression by definition is anything that holds you back, pushes you down, or keeps you from walking in freedom. And let's be clear, this oppression was the work of the enemy. This alone should challenge the idea that a Christian can't be affected by a demonic spirit. She wasn't "possessed" by the evil spirit, but a believer can be oppressed. If a covenant daughter could be under oppression for nearly two decades and still go unnoticed by religious leaders, how many believers today are silently struggling, attending church, loving the Lord, but still bound? Sometimes the greatest barrier to deliverance is the belief that we don't need it.

The Pharisees freed their bound animals on the Sabbath, but they questioned Jesus for freeing a child of God on His holy day. Jesus is the Lord of the Sabbath (Matthew 12:8). The Sabbath is subject to Him. He is not subject to the day He established. Instead, He is Lord over it. Deliverance can occur on any day of the week. In the context of the criticism that Jesus was getting, the Sabbath was a perfect day to see the Kingdom in operation.

The word "infirmity" typically refers to sickness, disease, or physical weakness. And to be clear, not every illness is caused by a demon. Some things require healing, while others require deliverance. In Mark chapter 1, we see Jesus doing both. First He delivers a man from an unclean spirit. Then a few verses later, He heals Simon's mother-in-law that was sick with a fever. The key is to know the difference. Since Jesus is both healer and deliverer, we can always ask the Lord how we should pray.

This story is a reminder that a believer can go to church, love God, and still have areas of bondage in their life. That doesn't mean they're possessed. But it does mean the enemy may be exerting an oppression that requires the authority of Jesus to break it.

Now that we've seen that a Christian can be oppressed (but not possessed) by a demon, let's take it one step further and talk about influence. Influence is the power to shape someone's behaviors, thoughts, decisions, or outcomes. From a spiritual perspective, influence can come from two places: Godly influence, like when the Holy Spirit gently leads us into truth, peace, and purpose. Or there's demonic influence, which usually works through the flesh, sin, deception, fear, confusion, pride, temptation, or any number of tactics to shift our thinking and throw us off course.

An example of both types of influences is found in Matthew chapter 16 NKJV, and it happens in two conversations involving the same person: Peter. In verse 15, Jesus asks His disciples an important question: "who do you say that I am?" Peter answers boldly in verse 16. "You are the Christ, the Son of the living God." Jesus tells Peter that this truth wasn't revealed by man but by His Father in Heaven. At that moment, Peter was under *Divine* influence, receiving and speaking a revelation straight from the Father.

Then, just a few verses later, still in the same chapter, we see things change. In verse 21 (NLT), Jesus begins to explain that He must suffer, be killed, and rise again on the third day. He's sharing the heart of the Gospel, the very plan of salvation. And how does Peter respond? In verse 22, he took Jesus and begins to rebuke Him, saying, "Heaven forbid, Lord, This will never happen to you!". Jesus immediately responds, not to Peter, but to the spirit behind the words: "Get behind Me, Satan! You are an offense to Me, for you are not mindful of the things of God, but the things of men" (Matthew 16:23, NKJV).

Peter wasn't possessed, but in that moment, his flesh minded response was influenced by the enemy—and Jesus called it out. This moment teaches us something critical. Even though we love Jesus and walk closely with Him, we can be influenced by wrong spirits if we are not discerning. That's why we must remain sensitive to the Holy Spirit and be led by Him in all that we say and do. With the help of the Holy Spirit, we can discern the things of God, reject what is false, and stay rooted in the things that are true.

SELF-REFLECTION QUESTIONS

1. Are there areas in my life where I'm saved but still struggling—places where I may need God's delivering power to walk in full freedom?

2. Am I open to the Holy Spirit revealing hidden ungodly influences in the way that I think, act, or behave?

SECTION III:
WHAT IS BONDAGE AND HOW TO BE FREE

WARFARE AND DELIVERANCE

TANYA D. NORWOOD

CHAPTER 4:
WHAT CIGARETTES TAUGHT ME ABOUT BONDAGE

Now that we've established that Christians can experience oppression and influence from demonic forces, let's delve into what it truly means to be in bondage. In Biblical terms, bondage refers to a state of being enslaved or controlled. Not just physically, but spiritually and emotionally by sin, fear, deception, or anything that keeps a person from walking in the freedom that Christ offers. Bondage can take many forms like addictions, intrusive anxious thoughts, irrational fears, or persistent shame, just to name a few. But allow me to share with you how I personally learned what it means to be in bondage.

First of all a clear sign of bondage is when a person feels compelled to engage in behaviors they don't truly want to do. No matter how harmful or destructive the behaviors may be, they feel powerless to stop. That was my experience with cigarettes.

I started smoking around the age of 14 or 15, thinking it was "cool". At first, it was purely social—I could take it or leave it without feeling dependent. By the time I graduated high school, I had quit altogether. At 19, I gave my life to the Lord. But during my college years, around age 21, I found myself smoking again.

To some this might not seem like a major issue, but it was through this struggle that I began to understand what bondage feels like. For me it was cigarettes, for others, it may be gambling, drug addiction, lust, alcoholism, pornography, masturbation—you name it. It's easy to look at someone caught in a cycle of sin or addiction and say "just stop", without realizing the depth of the spiritual battle they are facing.

The key thing to remember is that when someone is in bondage, they often experience intense internal pressure. Every time they try to resist, the urge becomes so overwhelming that they eventually give in—just to find relief. But that relief is fleeting, and it only strengthens the cycle of bondage. This isn't an excuse for sinful behavior, but it is a call to recognize the spiritual nature of the struggle (Ephesians 6:12). Understanding this reality should stir us to respond with compassion, prayer, and intercession, rather than judgement. Many people need help, and some are crying out silently. And the help that they need is a spiritual breakthrough.

Romans 6:16 (NLT) states, "**Don't you realize that you become the slave of whatever you choose to obey?** Satan fully understands this principle, which is why he works so hard to trap people in various forms of sin and bondage. His mission is always the same—to steal, kill, and destroy (John 10:10a). In addition to wanting to destroy our soul, the devil seeks to steal our peace, kill our purpose, and destroy our dreams, gifts, relationships, and God-given aspirations. Bondage is one of the devil's most effective tools to stagnate and destroy the life God has intended for us.

While not every struggle is the result of demonic influence, some issues stem from the flesh—such as self-indulgence, selfish ambition, or unchecked desires. When it's a matter of the flesh, we must crucify it. That means aligning our lives with God's will and practicing discipline, because we cannot cast out the flesh, we must put it to death (Galatians 5:24). However, if an evil spirit is involved, deliverance is necessary to break free from the pressure, harassment, and the behaviors that go against our will.

This is how bondage played out for me. Cigarettes were the first thing I thought about in the morning and the last thing before bed. They dominated my thoughts throughout the day. Knowing it was wrong didn't help me quit. The guilt and shame I felt didn't help either. It was a relentless cycle of trying to quit, succeeding for a few days, then succumbing to the pressure and starting again. Recurring cycles of bondage is also a sign of demonic activity.

This continued for years until one Sunday, something unexpected happened. At the end of a church service, the pastor invited anyone who wanted prayer to come forward. Without overthinking it, I went to the altar, but not specifically about cigarettes. The elders didn't ask for specific prayer requests; they simply laid hands on everyone at the altar, trusting that the Lord knew our needs. After the service, I didn't feel any different, and I never gave it a second thought. But the next morning, I woke up and realized I had no desire to smoke. This was miraculous to me, because as I previously mentioned, when you're in bondage, that thing will dominate your thoughts and desires. Yet, I woke up free. I experienced firsthand the power of prayer. The Lord Jesus had delivered me.

I wish I could say that was the end, but it wasn't. About three months later, the desire to smoke returned. I was confused. I knew God had delivered me, so why were the desires returning? Not understanding this, I began to fear I wouldn't be able to resist the temptation. And unfortunately, with the passing of time, I started smoking again.

I want to pause here. Often, when people think about deliverance, they expect someone to pray and make all their problems vanish forever. The Lord can absolutely do that! But we must remember that after deliverance, we have a responsibility to steward our deliverance when the temptation returns. Luke 4:13 KJV tells us that after tempting Jesus, Satan departed for a season. Seasons typically last a few months. If the devil tempted Jesus and came back after a season, he will certainly return to tempt us. I was free, but I had a responsibility to steward the freedom I had obtained.

I didn't realize it then, but the Lord was teaching me how to continue to walk in freedom. I'll discuss this more in the Chapter titled *Walking in Liberty*. Often, people get delivered, return home, and they don't renew their minds with God's Word or apply it. When the devil comes back to try and steal that freedom, they don't know how to respond. As a thief, Satan will try to steal the deliverance by manipulating a person's thoughts and emotions, hoping to create confusion and doubt to cause the person to doubt that the deliverance ever took place. I was truly delivered, but I had to learn to walk in that deliverance.

Later, I regained freedom. But this time, instead of yielding to temptation, I surrendered my will and yielded to the Lord. We cannot be "ignorant" of the devil's devices (2 Corinthians 2:11). He will try to tempt us and convince us that the very miracle we experienced never happened. The Lord could have delivered me in such a way that the desires never returned. And for some, that happens. However, I believe there was more the Lord wanted me to learn. I'm not saying He caused it, but He allowed it to help me grow and become established in a way that I would never go back to it again.

Overall, Jesus warned against returning to the bondage of sin. In John 5:14 KJV, after healing the man at the pool of Bethesda, Jesus told him "*Sin no more, lest a worse thing come unto thee*". When we understand why Jesus gave us this warning, we can understand why we should never give Satan a foothold. Engaging in sinful behavior without genuine repentance can open a door, giving the devil a "legal" right to enslave us in the very sin we are committing. This is why walking in repentance and obedience isn't only about holiness—it's also a reflection of freedom.

SELF-REFLECTION QUESTIONS

1. Are there any habits, fears, or continued past behaviors that are keeping me trapped and preventing me from walking in the freedom Christ offers?

2. What steps can I take to invite Jesus into any identified areas of bondage so I can experience His healing and be delivered?

CHAPTER 5:
THIS KIND GOETH NOT OUT BUT BY PRAYER AND FASTING

Fasting is one of many powerful tools God has given us. It's a spiritual weapon we can't afford to go without. I know conversations about giving up your favorite foods aren't exactly exciting for most people, but don't check out just yet. What you discover in this chapter might just surprise you.

You may already be familiar with Matthew 6:16 NLT, where Jesus begins with a striking phrase: *"When you fast."* Many of us know that when Jesus said "when," fasting wasn't optional, but expected. There will be times when we will need to push back the plate and press into His presence. Before I share a personal testimony with you, let's look at a powerful moment in Matthew

17:14–21. This passage shows just how critical fasting can be in spiritual battles.

> *"And when they were come to the multitude, there came to him a certain man, kneeling down to him, and saying, Lord, have mercy on my son: for he is lunatick, and sore vexed: for ofttimes he falleth into the fire, and oft into the water. And I brought him to thy disciples, and they could not cure him. Then Jesus answered and said, O faithless and perverse generation, how long shall I be with you? how long shall I suffer you? bring him hither to me. And Jesus rebuked the devil; and he departed out of him: and the child was cured from that very hour. Then came the disciples to Jesus apart, and said, Why could not we cast him out? And Jesus said unto them, Because of your unbelief: for verily I say unto you, If ye have faith as a grain of mustard seed, ye shall say unto this mountain, Remove hence to yonder place; and it shall remove; and nothing shall be impossible unto you. Howbeit this kind goeth not out but by prayer and fasting."*
>
> –MATTHEW 17:14-21 KJV

When the disciples asked Jesus why they couldn't cast out the demon as they had done before, Jesus' last statement was profound: *"This kind goeth not out but by prayer and fasting."* Prayer and fasting are not religious actions, but a humbled heart position. It doesn't manipulate God or force His hand, but it positions us to hear, receive, and respond to the Lord with clarity.

Like prayer, fasting is a weapon. Fasting accelerates things as a breakthrough in the realm of the spirit. Also as we commune with God we are transformed. Our fleshy nature is weakened, we are more sensitive to the Holy Spirit's leading, and our faith is increased.

Let's be clear, demons can be stubborn, and when you're up against that kind of resistance, your faith can be tested. In verse 20, Jesus answered by saying, "Because of your unbelief." Fasting and prayer can help to remove spiritual blockages like unbelief. If doubt is detected, the enemy won't flee easily; he'll push back and try to see if you believe what you say you believe. This is especially true when the warfare has been going on for a long time.

We see this same story told in Mark chapter 9, where the father tells Jesus that his son had been tormented since childhood. That means the young man was either grown or close to it by the time he encountered Jesus. The oppression had lasted for years. Imagine the toll, not just on the boy, but on the entire family. Over time, I am sure it looked hopeless.

As a reminder, I think it's worth noting again what Jesus said in Mark 16:17: *"These signs shall follow them that believe; in my name shall they cast out devils."* His *name alone* has the authority to drive out demons, but sometimes, our ability to walk in the reality of this truth *in faith* is hindered. Not because God is lacking, but rather because doubt, unbelief, fleshly perspectives or other distractions are in the way. Fasting helps us get past that.

When I began to understand this, I realized that some breakthroughs only happen through fasting and prayer. Jesus didn't just point to the problem; He gave the solution. A mustard seed of faith, coupled with prayer and fasting, can be explosive. That understanding became real to me through a personal experience.

Some years ago, a family member of mine was tormented by depression and suicidal thoughts. It was heavy, so heavy that no amount of comfort, logic, or encouragement seemed to help. He was in so much emotional pain that he started cutting himself to cope. The thought of him cutting himself for relief grieved my heart and it reminded me of Mark 5:5. In this chapter, it is recorded that there was a man that had an unclean spirit and he was living among the tombs. As he dwelled there, night and day he cried out and cut himself with stones. For me, I believed this incident of self-harm wasn't just emotional, it was spiritual. These scriptures made it clear that there was some type of demonic connection. And at the very least, a spirit of heaviness was involved (Isaiah 61:3 KJV).

When God revealed to me that an evil spirit was behind the hopelessness he was feeling, I knew I needed to intercede, and I felt drawn to fast. I had never prayed and fasted for something like this before. I wasn't sure how long I should fast or what exactly to do. A few days later, I came across a testimony from a woman who had interceded for a family member in a similar situation. She had fasted for seven days, and her family member was delivered. That was all the confirmation I needed. I committed to a seven-day fast.

During that week, I drank only tea and chicken broth once or twice a day. On the first day, I prayed to the Lord for his deliverance, then every day after that, I thanked Him for the breakthrough as if it had already happened.

Each day, I set aside time to pray and speak the Word over the situation. I didn't think or speak about anything else outside of that. Instead, my prayers were prayers of thanksgiving with declarations. I began with thank You Lord, that (fill in what you are believing for) is done!

The first few days weren't too bad. I was hungry periodically but managed by God's Grace. By day six, the hunger hit hard. I was tempted to give up. I had never fasted without food that long before, and everything in me wanted to quit. Yet deep down, I sensed that the intensity was a sign. A sign that the breakthrough was *close*. I leaned on God's grace and kept going.

After about a day or so after the fast ended, I received confirmation. His mother overheard him quietly say to himself, *"I will never do that to myself again."* With that report, my heart overflowed. I looked up and said, *"Lord, he decreed that over his own life, let it be unto him according to his words."* Praise the Lord that the last time he cut himself was years ago, and by God's grace, the repetitive desires to end his life ceased.

There are so many wonderful benefits of prayer and fasting but let me leave you with this thought for now. The enemy knows that if he can keep us comfortable, preoccupied, and "<u>full</u>" of all the wrong things, he has a better chance at keeping us distracted. So, let's trade food for consecration and indulgence for intercession, so that the devil's hold in our lives and the lives of others is broken.

SELF-REFLECTION QUESTIONS

1. How is the Holy Spirit leading me to pray and fast more intentionally in the face of spiritual opposition?

2. What distractions or comforts might I need to lay down in order to draw closer to God through prayer and fasting?

CHAPTER 6:

THERE IS POWER IN THE NAME OF JESUS

In chapter 2, we talked about the signs that follow believers. However, what is important to note is that Jesus said, "In My Name". The authority to cast out devils, heal the sick, raise the dead, etc. can only be done by the power and the authority of the Name of Jesus. Now, maybe you already knew that. I did too. I knew there was power in the Name of Jesus, but I hadn't considered what that power looked like in action. I didn't fully understand what that meant until I had a dream—that I believe was from the Lord.

The dream was brief, but the message was loud and clear. I found myself standing in an empty room in an unfamiliar house. The house was empty with the exception of this creature that stood about 4 or 5 feet away from me. Its skin was gray, leathery, and wrinkled. It was bald and short; it looked like something out of a sci-fi movie. Still, I didn't need an introduction. I *knew* it was a demon. As it looked at me, I felt led to speak: *"**Go in Jesus' name**."* So I said it, but here's the thing. It didn't come out loud. There was no shouting, no commanding tone. It was barely a whisper.

But that whisper came with *authority and power.* The demon reacted immediately. Cowering down and moving backwards, it threw its hands up in front of its face as if something had been thrown at it. I said it again, still softly, and the same thing happened. Each time I whispered, "Go in Jesus' name," the demon retreated. This continued until it backed itself up against the wall with no place to go. Then, I woke up.

When I woke up, I was puzzled. As I contemplated the details of the dream—*I was whispering.* I wasn't loud. I wasn't forceful. I wasn't even confident, but the Name of Jesus had all the force that was needed. That demon didn't fight back. He didn't resist. He knew he had no defense against the authority of the Name of Jesus. He had to go!

I believe the Lord was showing me something powerful through that dream. The victory isn't about how loud we are; it's in the authority we've been given. Now, there is nothing wrong with shouting, and there is a place for it. Shouting was part of the strategy for Gideon in Judges chapter 7, and for Joshua in Joshua chapter 6. But if the Lord did or did not give you those strategy instructions, remember the battle isn't about volume—it's about whose authority we are standing in. I once heard a minister say, *"You don't have to scream for demons to hear you."* It's the authority of the Name of Jesus that makes them tremble, not the volume of your voice.

If you've ever doubted the power and authority of the name of Jesus, allow the verses below to stir your faith. Let's take a moment to reflect on just how much authority, safety, and victory we've been given through His name.

Here are a few passages to meditate on:

(Our Foundation Scripture) "And these sign shall follow them that believe; In my name shall they cast out devils; they shall speak with new tongues; they shall take up serpents; and if they drink any deadly thing, it shall not hurt them; they shall lay hands on the sick, and they shall recover."
    –MARK 16:17-18 (KJV)

"The name of the LORD is a strong tower: the righteous runneth into it, and is safe."
    –PROVERBS 18:10 (KJV)

"For whosoever shall call upon the name of the Lord shall be saved."
    –ROMANS 10:13 (KJV)

"And it shall come to pass, that whosoever shall call on the name of the LORD shall be delivered."

　–JOEL 2:32 (KJV)

"And she shall bring forth a son, and thou shalt call his name JESUS: for he shall save his people from their sins."

　–MATTHEW 1:21 (KJV)

"That at the name of Jesus every knee should bow, of things in heaven, and things in earth, and things under the earth; and that every tongue should confess that Jesus Christ is Lord, to the glory of God the Father."

　–PHILIPPIANS 2:10-11 (KJV)

"Behold, a virgin shall be with child, and shall bring forth a son, and they shall call his name Emmanuel, which being interpreted is, God with us."

　–MATTHEW 1:23 (KJV)

"Behold, I give unto you power to tread on serpents and scorpions, and over all the power of the enemy: and nothing shall by any means hurt you. Notwithstanding in this rejoice not, that the spirits are subject unto you; but rather rejoice, because your names are written in heaven."

　–LUKE 10:19–20 (KJV)

SELF-REFLECTION QUESTIONS

1. Do I truly believe in the authority and power that is in the Name of Jesus.

2. Am I calling on the name of Jesus with faith and reverence for my situations, trusting that my victory is in His Name?

SECTION IV:
THE FIGHT IS IN THE MIND AND THE PRIZE IS THE HEART

WARFARE AND DELIVERANCE

TANYA D. NORWOOD

CHAPTER 7:
THE MIND IS
THE BATTLEFIELD

The Bible gives us clear instructions about how to protect and train our minds. In 1 Peter chapter 1:13 KJV, we're told to *gird up the loins of our minds* and to *be sober-minded.* Those phrases might sound old-fashioned, but they carry a powerful truth. We are called to be mentally prepared, spiritually alert, and ready for action in faith as we stand on the *Truth* that has been revealed to us by *God's Grace.*

Scripture also tells us to "*bring into captivity every thought to the obedience of Christ*" (2 Corinthians 10:4–6 KJV). And we should think on things that are true, honest, pure, lovely, of a good report, virtuous, and praiseworthy (Philippians 4:8 KJV). Over and over again, God emphasizes the importance of our thought life and how it shapes the way we live, speak, and believe. While many verses guide us in this area, Joshua 1:8 KJV summarizes them all for me. It says, *"This book of the law shall not depart out of thy mouth; but thou shalt meditate therein day and night, that thou mayest observe to do according to all that is written therein: for then thou shall make thy way prosperous, and then thou shalt have good success."*

To me, this scripture gives us a powerful blueprint of how to embrace the Bible: *speak it, think it, live it*—and then you'll *prosper* and *succeed*. When it comes to our thought life, we must know what the Word of God says and stick with it. If we don't, it's easy to get off course in the battle. The Holy Spirit is gracious to help us, and He will bring scriptures back to our remembrance, but we still carry the responsibility to take every thought captive and remain mindful of how we think.

EARLY IN MY WALK WITH CHRIST

As I shared earlier, I gave my life to Jesus when I was 19. I remember being so excited and passionate. I wanted everyone to know how deeply Jesus loved them and how He died to save them. But not long after my salvation, I was hit with a wave of intrusive thoughts. They questioned everything I believed. Thoughts like, "You don't believe that do you?" Or "the big-bang theory is how the world was created". These thoughts were not passive ideas, I felt them. The emotions behind them made the lies feel very real.

At that time, I didn't understand it was spiritual warfare. I was confused and trying to make sense of why I was thinking and feeling this way. Deep down, I *knew* those thoughts weren't true, but that didn't lessen the pressure. It was an intense three days of nonstop relentless thoughts of this nature. And while three days might not sound long, when your mind is under constant attack, it can feel like a lifetime.

Then suddenly, on the third day, it broke. I didn't see anything, but it felt like something had been gripping my head, and now suddenly it had to let go. If I had to describe it, the pressure felt like whatever had latched onto me could no longer maintain its grip and it flew away. Instantly, the thoughts stopped, the pressure lifted, and I felt like myself again.

Looking back, I realized the enemy was aggressively trying to get me to deny my faith. He saw an opening, which was my lack of understanding, and he tried to exploit it. But God kept me rooted in the truth, and that's the key. We don't need to know everything; we just need to know and hold on to the truth. It's the *truth* that makes us free (John 8:32 KJV). What I didn't know then was that this kind of attack was not going to be just a one-time thing.

THE MIND BATTLE INTENSIFIES

Around age 21, the intrusive thoughts came back, but this time, they were more disturbing. The enemy began firing blasphemous thoughts about God. I didn't want those thoughts, and they grieved me deeply. I found myself in constant anxiety and fear. I was heart-broken and confused. Why was this happening? I finally broke down and told my mother, who took me to speak with a local pastor. As much as I wanted the help, I was embarrassed and scared that I would be seen as crazy. Worse yet, I thought I had lost my salvation.

I sat in the pastor's office while my mom did most of the talking. I honestly don't remember what he said. I just remember that he wasn't sure what to do, and he didn't have an answer to give. This battle was spiritual and bigger than any human advice he could give me. Through it all, the Lord was with me. I had no idea that the Lord was about to show up and teach me how to fight this.

A SUPERNATURAL ENCOUNTER

One day, I was in my room crying out to the Lord, begging Him to forgive me for the thoughts that kept invading my mind. I didn't think I could take it any-more, and the Lord knew it. As I was heavily grieved in my heart and in tears, suddenly without warning, my entire bedroom was flooded with peace. The peace was so thick and so tangible, my tears literally dried up on my face. There was no evidence that I had been crying. With this experience I had and understanding of Revelation 21:4 KJV that says, "And God shall wipe away all tears from their eyes…". I then looked in the direction of the door in my bedroom. Even though I didn't see anyone there, I felt the presence of Jesus so strong, I knew He was standing inside my room. In that moment, I knew two things: I was still saved, and I was going to be okay.

The thoughts didn't stop immediately, but I had peace. I still didn't understand what was going on, but I soon learned that the Lord had a battle plan He wanted me to implement. Some days later, during another attack, the Holy Spirit gave me a strategy. He told me to *speak the opposite*. When a negative thought came against the character of God, I spoke the truth about the character of God out loud. I didn't relent. I was bold, fierce, and aggressive. Even though I could not physically see the enemy raging war against me, I obediently followed the orders the Holy Spirit had given me as my response to every attack. I didn't care how often the enemy came in an hour. If it were 100 times, he was going to be bombarded 100 times with the truth! I had no idea of how powerful this was. I just knew that within 24 hours, the thoughts had stopped.

ANOTHER BATTLE FOR A DEEPER REVELATION

After those two battles, I thought I had learned all that I needed to know. I had no idea that there was more that I needed to understand. This time I had to take what the Lord had taught me and apply it to every battle I faced. Not just selective battles here and there.

Some years later, I was experiencing a lot of anxiety, fear, and depression. I was going through a lot at that time and without realizing it I was not living by faith. Instead, I was allowing myself to live by my senses—according to what I saw, what I heard, and how I felt. Since I didn't know that I was walking by sight, my response was to brush things off, hoping the anxious and fearful thoughts would simply pass. But let me pause right here and say this, never respond to a spiritual attack with passivity. Ignoring it only gives it room to grow and affect your emotions. It begins with one unchallenged thought, and now your battle is not just about your thoughts, but also about what you feel. Satan loves to manipulate feelings through our thoughts because he knows if you dwell on it long enough or don't challenge it, you will begin to believe it's you. And that's exactly what happened to me.

At the time, I didn't realize what was happening. Even though I knew the negative feelings I was experiencing were not true, I stopped there. By brushing off the attack and assuming it would eventually fade, I did nothing—day after day, week after week, month after month. So by the time I finally began confronting the lies, a stronghold had already taken root, and it was firmly built like a fortified wall. This left me with anxiety, fear, and depression that no longer felt like external intrusions—now they felt like *me*. It began to feel like my identity.

One restless night, I got out of bed and began to pray. After a few minutes in prayer, I opened my Bible and landed in Proverbs chapter 23. When I read verse 7, which says, *"as he thinketh in his heart, so is he:"* I paused instantly. *"Wait"*, *I thought* we *think in our minds? But this says in the heart.* That changed everything. It made me realize that my true identity—my motives, beliefs, and attitudes—aren't shaped by fleeting thoughts in my mind, but by a deeper conviction in my heart.

Then the Lord led me to Luke 5:22 (NKJV), where Jesus asks the Scribes and Pharisees, *"Why are you reasoning in your hearts?"* Again, not the mind, but the heart. I began to see it clearly: not every thought that enters our mind is a direct reflection of our heart. This distinction is so important. Intrusive thoughts—even when they're intense or emotionally charged—are not who you are. They may pass through your mind, but that doesn't mean they've taken root in your heart. Recognizing this can be a powerful key to peace and freedom.

As I meditated further, I remembered a verse. Matthew 12:34b (NKJV) says, *"for out of the abundance of the heart the mouth speaks."* That verse reminded me of a powerful truth: if I wanted to know what was really in my heart, all I had to do was pay attention to my words. Whatever is overflowing in your heart will naturally come out through your mouth. So when the enemy whispered lies to my mind, I paid attention to my response. The truth I spoke in response to the lie was the truth that was rooted in my heart. That gave me peace—I could trust that my heart was still aligned with truth, even if my mind was under attack.

This shift in understanding changed everything for me. It helped me grasp why Scripture urges us to "gird up the loins of your mind" (1 Peter 1:13a KJV),—be mentally, spiritually, and even physically prepared for battle. Thoughts can't go unchallenged. And it helped me see the importance of being sober-minded, which means to think clearly, with discipline and self-control, unmoved by emotions, impulses, or distractions. Why? Because we don't want the wrong thoughts to enter into our heart.

During these seasons of learning the difference between mind battles and heart realities, I also came to understand why we can't be led by our senses. The enemy doesn't just target our thoughts—he also works through our emotions to reinforce his lie. When I give a word of advice to others who feel guilt or shame over thoughts they didn't invite, I tell them this: *Pay attention to what you're saying, not just what you're thinking and feeling.* Your words reflect your heart. And here's the bigger picture: God wants your heart. When we give Him our hearts, He molds them to look like Him.

Satan knows he can't simply take our hearts, but he'll try to access them through our minds. Because if he can get you to agree with his thoughts, he can influence your heart. And if he gains your heart, he begins shaping you into his image. The enemy's goal isn't only your peace of mind; it's your heart—that's the battle. That's why guarding it with truth is so important. Proverbs 4:23 NLT says, "Guard your heart above all else, for it determines the course of your life". This verse reminds us that the condition of our heart shapes everything in our lives, so we must be intentional about protecting it.

BUT WHAT IF MY HEART ISN'T RIGHT?

If you realize that your heart doesn't line up with the truth, don't be discouraged—you can begin replacing what is in your heart by thinking and speaking about what is true. Romans 12:2 urges us to *renew our minds,* and that means we must be intentional.

For example, there was a time when God revealed to me that I didn't have the right perspective of Him as my Father. My view of a "father" was how we see earthly dads. My parents separated when I was around 3 or 4, and without realizing it, that lack of a close relationship with my biological father had subconsciously affected my view of God. It wasn't that I didn't see Him as the Father, but I needed to grasp that He was not distant. I needed to embrace that not only does He love me, but He is interested in every detail of my life.

I was shocked to learn this. It was hard for me to embrace. Even though it was true, I couldn't see how this wrong perspective applied to me. Then one day God showed me three times within about 15-20 minutes the right perspective I needed to have. First I was on the phone with a dear sister in Christ and before we hung up she said "that's your Daddy girl". I was shocked when she said it because she had no idea what the Lord had revealed to me.

After the phone call, I decided to take a look at my email on my phone. At that time, I was subscribed to a well-known ministry that sent daily devotionals. When I opened the email, from what I can remember, it talked about "personally" calling and seeing God as your Father relationally. Again I was surprised. First the phone call, now the email.

After looking at the email, I decided to read a Christian book from my personal library. I didn't specifically have anything in mind that I wanted to read; so I randomly selected a book. With the book in hand, I randomly opened to a page in the middle and saw these words handwritten inside: "Abba Father". It was my handwriting, but I don't remember when or why I wrote it. And as far as I could tell, the written words had nothing to do with that chapter of the book. I knew instantly that I was divinely led to it, and it was not coincidental.

Realizing that I needed to change my perspective, I took the necessary steps to embed the truth into my heart. Whether I was in worship, prayer, or just giving thanks, I continually addressed God as "my" Father. Soon after, it not only became natural for me to say, but I began to wholeheartedly receive it and believe it.

Often I see myself as His little girl—His daughter. I now know, see, and feel His love for me and how He truly cares. He is actively involved in every aspect of my life. That's how I got the truth in my heart experientially and so can you. Just remember to repetitively renew your mind with the truth.

A WORD ABOUT STRONGHOLDS

Strongholds aren't demons, but they can be fortified by demons. When dealing with strongholds, we don't cast them out. We *cast them down*. A stronghold is a mental fortress built on lies and wrong thinking. That's why, as I stated earlier, it is important that we renew our minds.

Additionally, 2 Corinthians 10:3-6 KJV is our playbook. It reads: "For though we walk in the flesh, we do not war after the flesh: (for the weapons of our warfare *are* not carnal, but mighty through God to the pulling down of strongholds;) casting down imaginations, and every high thing that exalteth itself against the knowledge of God, and bringing into captivity every thought to the obedience of Christ;"

To take every thought captive, we must demolish it with the truth. We can't afford to let lies take up space in our minds unchecked. When we cast them down and speak God's truth, we're waging spiritual warfare. We're *punishing* those lies for trying to exalt themselves above the knowledge of God. And when our obedience is in place, the disobedience of those thoughts have no choice but to fall.

Lastly, it is important to note that it is essential that you know who you are in Christ. Your identity in Christ isn't just a truth—in battle, it's a *target*. One of Satan's most common strategies is to make you question who you are, and he doesn't always need a dramatic moment to do it. Sometimes all it takes is a thought, a whisper, or a single word of doubt. He tried this tactic with Jesus.

Right after the powerful moment when God the Father publicly declared, *"This is my beloved Son, in whom I am well pleased"* (Matthew 3:17b KJV). Jesus was led by the Holy Spirit into the wilderness to be tempted by the devil (Matthew 4:1). And what was the first strategy Satan came at Him with? Psychological warfare. He didn't deny who Jesus was, instead he tried to slip in a seed of doubt by saying, *"If You are the Son of God,… "* (Matthew 4:6 NKJV).

Satan recognized Jesus. He wasn't confused, but he was hoping *Jesus* would be. He hoped that if he could shake Jesus' confidence in His identity, Jesus might lose sight of His authority, purpose, and mission. And if the enemy tried that strategy on the Son of God Himself, you can be sure he'll try it with us too. That's why it's vital to stay rooted in the truth of who God says you are. No matter what lies, doubts, or temptations come your way, don't let go of your identity.

SELF-REFLECTION QUESTIONS

1. What thoughts am I consistently entertaining that may be shaping my beliefs more than the Word of God.

2. How often am I actively taking my thoughts captive and renewing my mind through Scripture?

CHAPTER 8:
THE HEART TEST

Some years ago, I was connected to a ministry with an international reach. I volunteered often, as I was drawn in by the richness of the sermons. The messages were unlike anything I'd encountered before. They were profound and deeply rooted in themes like forgiveness, the Kingdom of God, and the transformative power of early morning prayer. Though the ministry was nearly three hours away from where I lived, I made the trip a couple of times a year. When I wasn't there in person, I faithfully tuned in to their livestreams and conferences.

During services, powerful testimonies poured out, stories of miraculous healings, life-altering deliverances, and vivid dreams where people claimed to have encountered Jesus Christ Himself. The ministry felt like a spiritual oasis, and I genuinely believed it was helping me grow in my walk with the Lord.

But after about three years of involvement, accusations surfaced, painting a picture I couldn't ignore. The ministry leader, one that was highly esteemed, was accused of sexual misconduct involving multiple women, along with allegations of financial misuse. Soon after, disturbing reports came out about volunteer staff being verbally and physically abused, psychologically abused, spiritually manipulated, overworked, and deprived of basic physical and emotional needs.

Many loyal followers quickly dismissed the claims, labeling them as spiritual attacks or attempts to discredit a "true man of God." I didn't want to believe these claims, but it wasn't wise to ignore them either. I initially held onto the hope that if any of this were true, repentance and accountability would follow. But the more I listened, the more I learned, and the more disturbed I became.

The ministry leader denied all the offenses, offering explanations that seemed plausible—until I started hearing firsthand accounts from people I had served alongside. Some of them were his victims. Their stories were heart-wrenching. One by one, their testimonies aligned, and I could no longer ignore what was unfolding. I was stunned. Confused. Grieved. And left with two piercing questions:

1. *If the accusations were true, how could so many godly people that knew the truth defend and protect the ministry leader so fervently?*

2. *How could miracles, healings, and prophetic dreams still flow through a ministry associated with so much darkness?*

I turned to the Lord in prayer, desperate for clarity in the chaos. I asked Him how believers could knowingly stand by someone living in blatant sin who showed no sign of repentance. Not long after, I stumbled upon a teaching from the Book of Jonah, but the focus wasn't on Jonah himself; it was on the sailors.

God commanded Jonah to go to Nineveh to announce His judgment against the city. Jonah knew that God was gracious and merciful, and this led him to believe Nineveh might be spared if they repented. Jonah didn't want them to be saved, so instead Jonah fled in the opposite direction. He chose to board a ship to escape God's command. In response, the Lord sent a powerful wind over the sea, which caused a violent storm. So violent that it threatened to break the ship apart. The pagan sailors, unaware of Jonah's disobedience, found themselves caught in the middle of this storm, terrified and crying out to their gods in desperation.

Meanwhile, Jonah slept below deck. When they woke him, they wanted answers. After casting lots and a series of questions, Jonah confessed: *"I am a Hebrew; and I fear the LORD, the God of heaven, who made the sea and the dry land" (Jonah 1:9 NKJV).* Hearing this, the sailors were fearful. Jonah told them that he was the cause of the storm and that the storm would cease if they threw him overboard. Yet, they resisted. These men didn't worship the LORD, but they were afraid to harm a servant of the LORD, even though Jonah's disobedience was putting them in danger.

Instead, they tried to save Jonah, rowing hard toward land, but the storm only raged stronger. It wasn't until after they prayed to the LORD that they had the courage to throw him overboard. They asked to not to die because of Jonah's sins, and they asked to not be responsible for his death. After making those requests to the LORD, they threw Jonah into the sea. When Jonah went into the water, the storm ceased.

Then it all began to make sense to me. If you knowingly cling to someone who is walking in disobedience, you can suffer with them. Not because you committed the same sin, but by protecting or enabling them, you are aligning yourself with their rebellion. Naturally speaking, it's like being an accomplice to a crime.

The sailors were not guilty of Jonah's sin, but their survival depended on them "separating" themselves from Jonah's disobedience. The Lord allowed this teaching to show me what could happen to those who "knowingly" chose to continue to support someone in willful sin and unwilling to repent. I began to wonder if those that were still supporting the ministry truly understood the repercussions of their support

After this, I was still seeking an answer to my second question. How could miracles still happen? How could people continue to seemingly experience real healings, prophetic dream testimonies, and divine encounters under someone accused of such deep sin? The Lord answered—this time through Deuteronomy 13:1-3 (NKJV):

> *"If there arise among you a prophet or a dreamer of dreams, and he gives you a sign or a wonder, and the sign or the wonder comes to pass, of which he spoke to you, saying 'Let us go after other gods'—which you have not known—'and let us serve them,' you shall not listen to the words of that prophet or that dreamer of dreams, for the LORD your God is testing you to know whether you love the LORD your God with all your heart and with all your soul.*

This Scripture addressed the very thing I was wrestling with, signs, wonders, and dreams that came to pass. But here's the key: *those signs, wonders, and dreams are not endorsements.* Instead of looking at the signs and wonders, we must pay attention to who is being served.

What does it mean to "go after other gods?" It doesn't have to be a golden idol or a foreign deity. It can be anything we place above God, anything we refuse to surrender. It can be lust, money, power, pride, control, abuse, status, etc. They become gods when they dominate our decisions and dictate how we live our lives. So even though the perceived "work" of ministry was going forth, Godly devotion was lacking. Instead, idols of fornication, greed, pride, self-exaltation, deception, manipulation, and abuse were exalted.

God used that passage to remind me of the importance of truly *knowing* those who labor among us, versus trusting a polished public image (1 Thessalonians 5:12). In today's digital world, where anyone can curate a persona online, it's easy to be misled. But the Bible says, *"You will know them by their fruits."* (Matthew 7:16 NKJV). Not their gifts or charisma, but their fruits. So the real questions are: How do they treat people when no one is watching? Do they walk in love, humility, and accountability? Do their lives reflect the heart of God?

Lastly, the last sentence in verse 3 from Deuteronomy 13 shared an important warning, it says: *"For the LORD your God is testing you to know whether you love the LORD your God with all your heart and with all your soul"*. When all this happened, I couldn't help but ask God for clarity. Others, however, did not. I remember one woman saying, "I don't need to ask God about this Apostle. I know he's a man of God." That statement floored me! Not only because of her certainty, but because she didn't feel the need to ask God, even if she thought she was right. Her unwavering trust in a man, rather than in God's wisdom and authority, revealed the true position and allegiance of her heart.

In the end, this wasn't just a test of discernment. It was a test of love. Do we love the LORD our God with all our heart and soul? Do we trust His voice above our reasoning or admiration of others? Do we follow people, or do we follow Him? These are the questions that matter. And God, in His mercy, may allow these experiences so we can discern the fruit of who we follow and to self-examine our hearts to see where we are.

SELF-REFLECTION QUESTIONS

1. Am I enabling or overlooking sin in a minister's life out of loyalty or fear, rather than standing for truth and honoring God's standards?

2. Do I test spiritual messages and teachings against Scripture, or do I rely solely on charisma and emotion?

SECTION V:
HINDRANCES TO FREEDOM: DON'T GO BACK

WARFARE AND DELIVERANCE

TANYA D. NORWOOD

CHAPTER 9:
UNFORGIVENESS

Many things that block our spiritual freedom and healing fall under the category of "open doors." These open doors give the enemy legal access to torment us mentally, emotionally, and physically. Many of these access points will be identified and discussed in the next chapter. But, I want to spend some extra time on one doorway Satan has successively used to keep people bound: *Unforgiveness.*

When someone has wounded us deeply through betrayal, hurt, or actions that seem beyond forgiveness, our natural response is not to let it go. Forgiveness is often the furthest thing from our minds. Even so, offering forgiveness is the most deeply transformative step that we can take. It opens the door to our healing, releases us from inner torment, and aligns our hearts with God's.

Knowing this truth doesn't make it any easier. Instead, forgiveness can still feel like the hardest step to take. This chapter may initially be hard to swallow but hang in there until the end! I believe that by the end of this chapter, you will be so glad you stuck with it. Now let's take a moment to briefly state some of the manifestations of unforgiveness.

Unforgiveness can manifest in different ways for each person. For one person, it may be seething anger toward someone who wronged them. For another, it may be a subtle twinge of pain or tightness in the chest when a certain name is mentioned. Sometimes, it's hidden behind polite smiles toward someone we see every day yet silently resent. However, no matter how it shows up, it always results in the same thing: bondage. And you are unable or unwilling to let it go.

In Matthew chapter 18:21-22 NLT, we see an interesting conversation between Peter and Jesus. Peter begins with, "Lord, how often should I forgive someone who sins against me? Seven times?" Peter thought he was being generous. After all, Jewish law at the time only required forgiveness three times. But Jesus responded, "No, not seven times, but seventy times seven." That's 490 times! But Jesus wasn't telling Peter to carry around a calculator. Not that he would have been able to keep up with that anyway. Stop for a moment and imagine keeping a running tally on all the total offenses of every family member (parents, siblings, cousins, aunts, uncles, etc.), coworkers, church members and strangers you encounter (including when you offend yourself). Each individual would have their own personal tally or list of offensives so you could keep track of them. However, Jesus was teaching that forgiveness *is not* something we count. Every act of forgiveness resets the count to zero, and in a practical sense, that is much easier than carrying a calculator. It gives the offender a clean slate. It's not based on what we think they deserve, instead we have decided to release them.

As we continue to read Matthew chapter 18, we see Jesus continuing to disciple Peter with a parable. He shares that there was a man who owed an unfathomable debt to a king. Over a billion dollars in today's currency. An estimation of 200,000 years of work. The man begged for mercy, and the king forgave the entire debt. However, that same man turned around and demanded repayment from someone who owed him a significantly lesser amount, about six thousand dollars in today's currency, or an estimation to 100 days of work. When the man asked for more time to pay him back, no mercy was given; he threw him in jail. He was to remain there until his debt was paid in full, but 200,000 years of work is impossible to pay back.

When the king found out, he was furious. He called the unmerciful man a wicked servant because he was shown and given mercy but wasn't willing to extend it to someone else. The parable ends with the man being handed over to the tormentors. Think about that for a moment. Unforgiveness opens the door to being tormented. A tormentor is a person who inflicts severe mental and physical suffering on someone else. It can come in the form of distress, emotional instability, oppression, seething anger, wrath over what was done, an increasingly hardened heart of bitterness, and even devastating health issues to name a few. With this perspective, we can see how prosperous it is for us to forgive others versus not letting it go.

Jesus forgave us so that we can walk in the liberty and freedom of His salvation. He wants us to be free and turn that same forgiveness He gave us toward others. At the end of the parable, Jesus gave a sobering truth. He said, "That's what my heavenly Father will do to you (deliver you to the tormentors) if you refuse to forgive your brothers and sisters from your heart" (Matthew 18:35, NLT).

Reading this, you may be thinking, how can I forgive the abuse, betrayal, slander, and the way the person destroyed my life? These are valid questions, but please keep in mind that you can't forgive without the help of the Lord.

The first step is to decide to forgive and watch the Lord do the rest. Forgiveness is not a feeling; it is a decision. One of the biggest misconceptions about forgiveness is that we need to feel like forgiving to forgive. When, actually, it's a decision to obey God. A decision to release someone from the debt they owe us, even if they never apologize.

Making that choice may not take the pain away instantly, but it opens the door for God to begin the healing process. When we forgive, we're not excusing the wrong. We're saying, "God, I trust You with what was done. I won't carry this anymore."

MY JOURNEY

Like many of you I have been betrayed, lied to, hurt, rejected, and abused. But I want to share with you a time when the Lord first taught me how important it is to forgive. This experience that I will share, helped me to forgive past painful experiences I have had with others, as well as how to correctly respond to any offenses today.

Some years ago, I was deeply committed to a church I loved, but I began to feel overlooked and undervalued. New and old members were celebrated and embraced, while I felt invisible. People would ask me, "Why are you still there? They don't recognize you." I would respond, "I'm not doing what I do for recognition." But quietly, the rejection hurt. The hurt turned into anger and frustration, then to offense. Before I knew it, I was festering in unforgiveness.

One day, while driving and replaying the pain in my mind, the Lord interrupted my thoughts and said something I will never forget: "You do not have a right to be offended." When I heard this, I immediately thought of my response, thinking the Lord would see my point of view if I responded with, "I didn't do anything." However, before I could inhale so that I could speak those four words out of my mouth, the Lord responded with, "Even if you didn't do anything, you still don't have the right to be offended." That moment humbled me instantly. I realized that it didn't matter how "innocent" I thought I was; I still didn't have a right to be offended. God wasn't minimizing my pain. He was correcting my perspective.

I knew I couldn't change my heart on my own. So I asked the Lord to help me.

Soon after, I heard a testimony about someone who overcame offense by praying daily for those who hurt him. I thought, *"I don't want to do that,"* but I humbled myself and prayed anyway. I wrote down a list of names and started praying for them. At first, it was quick, awkward, and emotionless. But within a couple of days or so, God began to soften my heart. Before long, I wasn't praying out of duty—I was praying with tears of compassion. In those moments, I gained a deeper understanding of Matthew 5:44 NKJV, "Pray for those who spitefully use you and persecute you". Basically, pray for your enemies. It is important to note that I didn't see the people in the church as my enemies. But if we are instructed to love and pray for our enemies, how much more do we need to do the same for our brothers and sisters that have offended us.

When I began to understand this, I quickly found out that the Lord still had more He wanted me to learn. Once we truly forgive someone, we could stop there. Or we can allow love and mercy to take it a step further. When we extend love and mercy to the person who wronged us, and they respond, it disarms the enemy. How? Now instead of having one softened heart there are two. Now the enemy hasn't lost once, but twice. He no longer has power over you to be bound in bitterness, and he no longer has power over them to continue the offense. Forgiveness becomes a chain reaction. First it sets *you* free, then it creates a path for *others* to be free as well. Forgiveness allows healing while engaging in warfare at the same time. It's how we take ground back from the enemy, one heart at a time.

We can make forgiveness complicated when we try to dictate what it should look and feel like. Allow me to clarify a few things that are important to remember. First of all, forgiveness doesn't always mean reconciliation. Forgiving someone doesn't always mean you will or should reconcile with a person. You can forgive a person without continuing a relationship, especially if it is unsafe, unhealthy, or abusive. Forgiveness is about freeing your heart. You can set healthy boundaries while still choosing to walk in love and forgiveness.

Secondly, we may have to forgive without an apology. We may never hear "I'm sorry." However, we forgive not because they asked, but because Jesus forgave us.

Sometimes we are waiting painfully for God's justice to show up, especially when someone has done wrong and has not faced any consequences. From the outside, it can look like nothing is ever going to happen, like God is silent or indifferent. But what we must remember is this: God sees far deeper than we do. He knows the condition of every heart. He knows whether that person will one day turn and truly repent or not. And because of that, He often extends mercy. Not because He's ignoring wrong-doing, but because He's giving space for repentance, just like He has done for each of us. His justice is never late; it's perfectly timed, perfectly wise, and always balanced with His incredible mercy. The same patience he offers to us, He offers to others too.

Third, sometimes we hold off on forgiving because we're waiting to *feel* ready. We think the right emotion has to show up first. Like feelings of peace, relief, or even love—but what we don't realize is that feelings are fluid. They can shift with time and perspective. And if we wait for our emotions or moods to line up perfectly before we forgive, we can stay stuck for a long time. Forgiveness doesn't begin with a feeling—it begins with faith. It starts with a choice, not an emotion. It's often uncomfortable at first. It may even feel forced, but that's okay, because it's a process, not an all encompassing moment. As we take steps, sometimes small, our heart begins to follow. Eventually, the emotions that felt so resistant begin to soften, and our feelings start to align with the decision we have made. Also, keep in mind that the devil is watching. He may try to bring back old emotions. When this happens, declare, "I've already forgiven them. I will not rehearse the pain, I will rest in God's peace."

Fourth, it's not our job to make sure someone *feels* the weight of the pain they caused us. As much as we may want them to understand the hurt, it's not our responsibility to make them experience consequences. God sees everything—every wound, every word, every wrong—and He knows exactly how to deal with it. Romans 12:17-19 (NLT) speaks directly to this. It says, *"Never pay back evil with more evil. Do things in such a way that everyone can see you are honorable. Do all that you can to live in peace with everyone. Dear friends, never take revenge. Leave that to the righteous anger of God. For the Scriptures say, 'I will take revenge; I will pay them back,' says the LORD."*

The King James Version puts it this way: *"Vengeance is **MINE**; I will repay, saith the Lord"* (emphasis mine). These verses remind us of something powerful: God never told us to carry out justice on our own. When we step in to get revenge, we step into territory that belongs to Him alone. It's like someone once said, *"When we take revenge, we're stealing from God."* He didn't say vengeance was *ours* to manage—He said it was *His*.

We see this principle clearly in the life of David. When Saul was actively trying to kill him, David had more than one opportunity to take revenge, but he didn't. Even when Saul was right within his grasp, David chose restraint. In I Samuel 24:12 NLT David says, "May the LORD judge between us. Perhaps the LORD will punish you for what you are trying to do to me, but I will never harm you". David didn't excuse Saul's actions or pretend they weren't wrong. Instead he recognized that the same God who anointed Saul as king was fully capable of dealing with Saul's behavior.

That puts us at a crossroads: Are we going to trust that *He* is the righteous judge, or are we going to try to take that role for ourselves? Our hope and prayer should always be for the offender to repent, turn to God and be changed. God is more than capable of dealing with the situation in His perfect wisdom, justice, and timing. Letting go of revenge doesn't mean the offense didn't matter; it means we're choosing to place it in the hands of the only One who can handle it righteously. And in doing so, we not only honor God but also free ourselves from becoming bitter.

Allow me to take a pause for a moment and share that I am not saying people should not be held accountable. There are laws in place to report and handle such situations (e.g. theft, abuse, endangerment, murder), and Biblically Jesus instructs us to judge with "righteous judgement" (John 7:24 KJV). To judge righteously, we evaluate the situations, actions, and people with truth, fairness, accountability, and Godly discernment instead of biases, hypocrisy, and a "I will make you pay" mentality.

The fifth point, forgiving others also includes forgiving yourself. Sometimes it is hard to forgive ourselves. Instead, we replay our failures, regret our decisions, and beat ourselves up over things God has already forgiven. Guilt and shame do not come from God. The Holy Spirit brings conviction, not to condemn us, but to guide us toward transformation. When He convicts us, He also reveals a way forward—a path to change and healing. In contrast, condemnation holds us back, keeping us stuck in the past. It doesn't lead to freedom; it traps us—so we don't move forward.

Lastly, let's be honest with ourselves, this part isn't always easy to admit, but there are times in our walk when we may find that we need to forgive God. Now, to be clear, God has never wronged us. He is perfect, just, and faithful in all His ways. But from our human perspective, especially in the midst of pain, grief, or unanswered questions, it can *feel* like God let us down.

When we go through deep hurts, whether it's the loss of a loved one, a dream that never came to pass, betrayal we didn't expect, or a prayer we were desperately hoping God would answer, we might begin to question His goodness, His fairness, or even His love for us. These moments can quietly plant disappointment, confusion, or resentment in our hearts. Without realizing it, we may begin to pull away from Him. We go through the motions—attending church, reading scripture—but inside, there's a distance, a wound. We may silently ask:

- *Lord, why didn't You stop it?*
- *Why did You allow that to happen to me?*
- *Where were You when I needed You most?*

Here's the comforting truth: God can handle your honesty. He is not afraid of your questions. He won't turn you away for expressing your pain, doubts, or confusion. He invites you to bring it all to Him, not so He can scold you, but so He can heal you.

Psalm 34:18 NLT tells us, *"The LORD is close to the brokenhearted he rescues those whose spirits are crushed."* That means even when your heart is broken *because* of how you feel, He is right there.

When you come to Him with a sincere heart saying "God, I don't understand why this happened," it's in that place of raw honesty that God can restore what was broken. He gently helps you to see things from His perspective, and over time, what once felt like betrayal becomes a part of your testimony, where pain was exchanged for healing.

Don't carry silent resentment. Don't let the unanswered "why" distance you from the only One who can truly bring healing. Talk to Him. Invite Him into your questions. Let Him walk you through your hurt. He is a good Father, and

He is not offended by your pain; He wants to redeem it by turning it into restoration and strength.

If I could sum up this entire chapter with a visual, it would look like this: Imagine your heart as a garden. When someone offends or wounds you, and especially when you don't deal with it, that offense becomes a seed. The soil of your heart, whether you realize it or not, receives it. Left unattended, that seed doesn't just sit there; it *grows*. It takes root. And over time, it begins to produce fruit, but not the kind you want. This fruit can show up as offense, simmering anger, bitterness, or even deep resentment and hatred. The Bible calls bitterness poison, and more specifically, a poisonous root (Hebrews 12:15 NLT). Something that starts hidden but spreads. It not only affects you but also *corrupts others* around you. Like poison, it contaminates everything it touches.

Here's where many of us miss it: We try to clean up the *fruit* without ever getting to the *root*. We might say things like, "I'll just be nicer," or "I'll let it go," while relying on our "own" strength, trying to fix what's happening on the surface. It's like tugging on a weed that is rooted in dry compacted soil. You might break off a few branches. You might even tear off the top, but the root stays firmly in place, hidden but alive, and it will grow back. It's also like climbing a ladder and picking all the visible fruit off a tree but leaving the tree untouched. The tree remains, and sooner or later, the same fruit grows back.

But when we choose to forgive, everything changes. Forgiveness invites God into the soil. It softens what was once hard. And suddenly, the root that seemed impossible to move starts to loosen. God, the Master Gardener, doesn't just remove the offense; He begins to heal the ground. He waters it with grace, nurtures it with truth, and restores it with His love. And as He tends to your heart, He doesn't just pull up the pain, but also transforms the very place where it was planted.

That's why, after true forgiveness and healing, you can look back on the same situation and see it *differently*. You're no longer looking through the lens of pain or betrayal—you're seeing through the eyes of God, from a heart that's been healed, not hardened. Forgiveness isn't weakness; it's warfare.

SELF-REFLECTION QUESTIONS:

1. Is there someone you need to forgive today?

2. Do you need to forgive yourself?

3. Do you need to forgive God?

Let go of the past hurts that are still controlling your emotions today.

Let's Pray

Dear Lord Jesus,

Thank You for Your Word and the Wisdom You've given me to understand the true power of forgiveness. Thank You for revealing the enemy's tactics so that I am no longer unaware of his schemes against me. I am grateful for the gift of repentance and the incredible gift of forgiveness.

Right now I repent for holding on to unforgiveness. I release myself and every person You bring to my heart to forgive (pause and forgive whoever the Lord brings to mind). I forgive each one of them for what they did to me; I forgive myself and forgive me if I am holding anything against You. I release everyone that has offended me. I put them into Your hands. Lord deliver me, make me free and heal my heart. Help me to use this experience as a testimony of Your perfect love to help and encourage others. In addition to healing my heart, Lord, I ask that You would heal my body, my mind, my emotions, my soul, and my relationships. Thank You, as I ask all these blessings in Your Name, amen.

CHAPTER 10:
OPEN DOORS

Physically and spiritually, doors signify transition, and they represent a point of access. Spiritually, an open door to God is an invitation for us to enter His presence, promises, and His direction for our lives. In John 10:9 KJV, Jesus declares, "I am the door," offering salvation to all who enter through Him. On the other hand, opening a door to the enemy—whether through sin, compromise, or spiritual blindness, Satan gains "legal" access to influence our lives. In Genesis 4:7 (NLT), God warned Cain that sin is crouching at the door. This gives us a vivid picture of how sin was eager to come in and take control. In that moment, Cain's unbridled emotions were not subdued, which resulted in sin opening the door, giving access to a tragic act of murder.

When a door is closed, it symbolizes a boundary, protection, and a defense. Spiritually, closing the door blocks the enemy from influencing us. Closing the door on Satan not only indicates a boundary for protection; it also represents the willingness to live by God's Word and His commands. The enemy doesn't always try to force his way in. Instead, he will try to manipulate circumstances and situations and then wait for an opening. Let's explore some of the ways Satan gains access and how we can resist him.

A LACK OF REPENTANCE

Repentance is a *vital* part of the Christian Walk. It's not just an initial act when we first come to Christ—it's an ongoing practice of turning away from sin and turning our hearts toward God. When someone is seeking deliverance from demonic oppression but refuses to repent of the sin that opened the door, they are unknowingly allowing the devil to keep legal access into their life. How? Because unrepented sin gives the devil a foothold—a legal right to remain and continue his destructive work.

Repentance means to change your heart, mind, and behavior toward sin—turning away from it and surrendering fully to God. If it's a struggle, ask God to help you (He already knows). With His help, you can experience true repentance that leads to spiritual restoration that also closes the door to demonic influences.

PRIDE

Pride is often subtle, yet it is incredibly destructive. Proverbs 16:18 NLT says, "Pride goes before destruction and haughtiness before a fall". Also, James 4:6 NLT says, "God opposes the proud but gives grace to the humble". So not only can pride destroy us, but it will also cause God to oppose us. To oppose something means you are not in agreement with it, and you will resist it.

Pride will distort our perspectives. When in operation, it silences conviction, resists correction, and blocks the flow of Godly wisdom. It causes us to lean on our own understanding rather than trusting in God.

Satan was cast down out of heaven because of pride. His rebellion coupled with his desire to elevate himself above God led to his fall (Isaiah 14:12-15). When we entertain pride, it can lead to rebellion. We must be careful that we do not unknowingly align ourselves with it. Humility brings us back into alignment with God. At its core, it means coming into agreement with Him—saying, "God, You know best. I choose Your way over mine." When we humble ourselves before Him, we close the door to pride and make room for His wisdom, peace, and grace. In that posture, we become vessels that God can shape and guide.

UNFORGIVENESS

Unforgiveness was discussed at length in the previous chapter, so I will only highlight a few things here. Unforgiveness is one of the most utilized tools that the devil uses to gain access and create havoc in our lives. And it is his most utilized tool to block deliverance. *Demons will not leave when a person refuses to forgive and unforgiveness can keep us out of the Kingdom of God.* The Bible is clear that unforgiveness (like all other open doors) gives the enemy a foothold (Ephesians 4:27 NLT). A foothold doesn't start as a full-blown takeover, but it gives just enough space for the enemy to get a grip. Similar to rock climbers who establish a secure place to grip their footing, or a robber who has successfully put his foot in the doorway before you close the door. Once Satan has access, he won't stop with a small spot in the corner, he wants to take over the entire house. And unforgiveness can be that open door.

IDOLATRY AND WITCHCRAFT:

Idolatry isn't just about statues or ancient altars— it's any form of worship, devotion, or deep reverence given to something or someone other than God. It can be obvious, such as bowing to false gods, or subtle and deceptive, like chasing after money, status, relationships, or even our own image. The enemy thrives in these distractions. Why? Because idolatry shifts our affection, focus, and dependency away from God, giving Satan room to influence our heart and our decisions.

Similarly, witchcraft and occult practices—whether it's divination, tarot card readings, Ouija boards, or crystals—these things are not spiritually neutral. These rituals, no matter how harmless they seem, are rooted in manipulation, control, and demonic power. Deuteronomy 18:10-12a (NLT) says: "*For example, never sacrifice your son or daughter as a burnt offering. And do not let your people practice fortune-telling, or use sorcery, or interpret omens, or engage in witchcraft, or cast spells, or function as mediums or psychics, or call forth the spirits of the dead. Anyone who does these things is detestable to the Lord.*"

At the core, these practices involve seeking supernatural knowledge, power, and control from demonic sources. Satan has led countless to believe that following his ways leads to a position of power, never revealing that the position came with a price. The cost? Access into their lives to wreak havoc (kill, steal, and destroy) and ultimately destroy their soul and the souls of future generations.

GENERATIONAL CURSES

Generational curses are a serious yet often misunderstood strategy that the enemy uses. These curses aren't just random hardships; they are repeated patterns of misfortune in a family. They are spiritual strongholds that can be passed down through family bloodlines due to sins like idolatry, rebellion, or involvement in the occult. What makes them especially dangerous is that they don't just affect one person—they can ripple through multiple generations, shaping patterns of behavior, oppression, and bondage. Some examples include ongoing illnesses without an explanation, cycles of financial hardships, chronic rebellion against authority, violent behaviors, addictions, chronic broken relationship cycles, abusive behaviors, cycles of accidents that are unusual in nature, a family pattern of sudden untimely deaths, or patterns of constant failure. If the generational curses are not broken, they will continue to affect future generations.

Through repentance and faith, we are no longer bound by the sins of our ancestors, and Galatians 3:13-14 reminds us that Christ redeemed us from the curse of the law, being made a curse for us. So we are not destined to carry what our forefathers didn't overcome. However, we may be experiencing the consequences of the sins that were committed by them. God is merciful and forgiving, but He is also just. If we do not repent for the sins of idolatry, the consequences can affect our descendants down to the third and fourth generation (Deuteronomy 5:7-10).

So to break a generational curse, we must be intentional. It begins with repentance—not only for our sins but also for the sins committed in our family line. After repentance, we must then renounce those sins that were committed (e.g. idolatry, occult, etc.) and ask the Lord to remove the curse. It's simple, through repentance and prayer, those doors can be closed! Satan's mission to kill, steal, and destroy has not changed. He wants us and our children. So let's take a stance and say —no, it stops here.

Prayer to Break Generational Curses

Heavenly Father,

I come before You in the name of Jesus Christ. I thank You that through the blood of Jesus, I am redeemed from every curse, past, present, and future. You are the God who sees every hidden thing, and nothing is too hard for You to deliver, heal, and restore.

Right now, I acknowledge the sins and iniquities committed by me and by my ancestors, whether knowingly or unknowingly, sins of idolatry, rebellion, witchcraft, sexual immorality, bloodshed, and any agreements made with darkness. Holy Spirit, I ask that you would bring to my attention any hidden sins that I need to confess (pause and confess whatever the Holy Spirit brings to you). I confess these sins before You. I ask for Your mercy and forgiveness for me and over both sides of my family, back to the third and fourth generation or further, if that is what is needed for me and my children to be free.

I now renounce every generational curse, stronghold, or spiritual claim the enemy has tried to establish

*through those sins. I break every chain in Jesus' name.
I cancel every assignment of darkness that was passed
down through my bloodline and declare that it ends
with me. By the authority of the Lord Jesus Christ, I
close every door that was once open to the enemy, and
I apply the blood of Jesus over my life, my family, and
future generations.*

*Holy Spirit, I invite You into every broken place. I ask
that You would restore what was stolen. Heal what
was wounded. And renew what has been distorted by
generations of sin. From this moment forward, I declare
that I belong to Jesus Christ alone. I am a new creation.
The old has passed, and the new has come. I will walk
in the inheritance of the Kingdom—boldly, freely, and
completely whole. And I declare that my children and
their children will live under the blessings of the Lord,
not the curses of the past. In Jesus' mighty name—Amen.*

NEW AGE

The New Age movement is a broad, modern spiritual philosophy that blends elements from various religions, belief systems, and occult practices. It promotes the idea that everything in the universe is connected by a universal energy, and that individuals can attain spiritual enlightenment by tapping into this energy. Core beliefs often include the idea that each person is "divine," that all spiritual paths lead to the same truth, that positive thinking shapes reality, and that death is not the end. For spiritual insight or guidance, New Age practices commonly turn to tools such as crystals, astrology, tarot cards, spirit guides, and energy healing that is believed to unlock hidden spiritual powers.

Fundamentally, New Age replaces biblical truth by denying that Jesus is the only way to God the Father (John 14:6). Instead it is a mix of self-worship, false spirituality, and occult practices, disguised as light, positivity, or healing. When in all actuality, it opens doors to deception and demonic influence.

COMMON NEW AGE BUZZWORDS:

- Manifesting / Manifest what you want – Name it, claim it—attract abundance.

- Vibrations - Raising your vibe. Good vibes only, high-frequency energy.

- The Universe - The universe is aligning things for you instead of God.

- Energy Healing - Reiki, chakra balancing, aura cleansing.

- Crystals - Used for healing, protection, or positive energy.

- Spirit Guides /Ascended Masters - Spirits supposedly helping you but are actually familiar spirits (demons).

- Third Eye Awakening - Spiritual "enlighten-ment" tied to occult practices.

- Meditation - Not biblical meditation on God's Word but emptying your mind to be "one with the universe".

- Horoscopes / Astrology – Putting faith in the stars or birth dates to predict your future.

- Law of Attraction - Teaching that positive thoughts alone can control your destiny.

- Inner Divinity / Higher Self - Believing there's a "god" within you that you must unlock.

- Past Life Regression - Belief in reincarnation—and that you can access memories of past lives.

- Mindfulness - Secular meditation practices to gain mental peace apart from Christ.

- Oneness / Universal Consciousness - Claiming all humans, nature, and spiritual beings are one divine force.

It is important to understand that terms like—"heal-ing," "abundance," or "good energy" may sound positive on the surface. However, many of these concepts can quietly redirect our trust toward ourselves, spiritual energy, or other forces that are not from God. Instead of honoring the Lord, they elevate self, the universe, or hidden knowledge as if they were divine. But as Exodus 20:3 NKJV says, *"You shall have no other gods before*

Me". This command is more than a rule—it's a safeguard. New Age beliefs wrapped in spiritual language can lead us away from the one true God. He is our only source—faithful, trustworthy, and powerful enough to save and restore.

ENTERTAINMENT AND MEDIA:

In today's society, entertainment and media are among the most powerful influences shaping our thoughts and behaviors. Music, movies, TV shows, and even video games often contain themes of violence, sexual immorality, and rebellion. This type of media is widely accepted as entertainment, but its content can subtly shape our worldview and attitudes, often reflecting and promoting demonic ideologies.

Satan uses these platforms to subtly introduce themes of rebellion, lust, fear, and witchcraft. For example, the music beats often have a hook and a frequency for a purpose. The goal is to allow the sounds to manipulate emotions while also drawing you in to speak over yourself a declarative narrative. Pay attention to the words. Do they speak life or death, good or bad? Do the words encourage or tear down? It's easy to "excuse" the lyrics because of the beat, not realizing that the words spoken have opened a door. If we are not vigilant, the message in the music can not only influence how we think, speak, and behave, but it can also open the door to demonic influence.

Discernment is key. We need it to monitor what we consume through media. Philippians 4:8 urges us to focus on things that are pure, lovely, and praiseworthy. Not all entertainment is inherently evil, but we must be careful not to expose ourselves to harmful influences that invite spiritual compromise. Choose movies, music, books, and games that don't compromise your faith; ones that promote a healthy, Godly lifestyle.

ADDICTIONS:

Addictions are a strong form of bondage, one that enslaves a person to a substance, behavior, or habit. Earlier in this book, we talked about how crucial it is to monitor our thoughts because an unmonitored thought life can shape our actions, emotions, and even our spiritual posture. But if our thinking becomes clouded or altered by a substance, whether it's drugs, alcohol, or anything that dulls our senses, it becomes incredibly difficult to stay mentally alert and engaged in *any* kind of battle.

Think of it like this: you can't effectively fight physically if your vision is blurred or your reflexes are delayed. In the same way, spiritually when our minds are compromised, our discernment weakens, our awareness drops, and our spiritual defenses are lowered. The enemy thrives in those moments, slipping in thoughts and temptations that we normally resist when fully sober and spiritually sharp. A clear mind is a guarded mind—ready to discern, respond, and stand firm. That's why protecting our mental and spiritual clarity is not just wise; it's *warfare* (2 Corinthians 10:4-5).

Additionally, the devil uses addictions to keep people trapped in cycles of despair and hopelessness. Some examples are drugs, alcohol, gambling, and pornography. They start off enjoyably to the flesh but eventually it comes to a place where the person feels guilt and shame. Not only will an addiction open the door to oppression, but it is also a form of idolatry. We are meant to turn to Jesus for comfort, peace, and strength, but an addiction will invite you to look elsewhere.

One of the most addictive behaviors known today is digital platforms. How often have you found yourself or someone else scrolling aimlessly on a social media platform. It is designed to be a distraction; it stifles creativity and promotes "wasting time". And as with any addiction, deliverance and denying our flesh is crucial as it leads to us turning away from the vice that has stolen our adoration and affection and properly placing it upon the Lord.

SEXUAL IMMORALITY

In the world today, discussions about sexual purity may seem outdated or out of touch. Yet, the Bible remains timeless. What was true in the past holds true today. In 1 Corinthians 6:18 (NLT), Paul warns: *"Run from sexual sin! No other sin so clearly affects the body as this one does. For sexual immorality is a sin against your own body."* The seriousness of this warning is clear because outside of marriage, sexual intimacy can cause you to become spiritually and emotionally connected with another person. Just as sexually transmitted diseases can be passed between individuals physically, demonic oppression influencing one person can also open the door for it to also oppress you.

I heard a testimony of a young man that stated that *immediately* after he was intimate with a woman that was not his wife, his attitude changed. He turned his hat backwards on his head and he allowed his pants to sag. These behaviors caught his attention, because he never carried himself that way before. Later that day the young man called the young lady he had been with and asked her if she had ever slept with thugs. She said yes. In that moment he realized that he not only connected to her but with everyone she had slept with. Please note that I am not saying that everyone that turns their hat backwards or sags their pants is a thug. People follow fashion trends for a variety of reasons. This testimony is just an example that visually expresses how what is tied to one person can also be tied to you.

Additionally, I am sure we have all seen how sexual immorality (fornication, adultery, lust, and perversion) can destroy relationships, homes and families. Just as it is important to protect and maintain our God ordained relationships, we must also be diligent to cut off the ungodly ones—that create ungodly soul ties.

One way an ungodly soul tie is formed is through sexual activity. Sexual intimacy is God's design as something special between a man and a woman that is married to each other. Sex outside of His design will result with the person developing a deep connection emotionally and spiritually with someone that is not their spouse. The number of partners can be a direct correlation to the number of soul ties formed. These deep bonds can linger and influence your life long after the ungodly relationship has ended. If not severed in prayer, they can disrupt your current relationships and your personal well-being.

To break a soul tie, ask the Lord to reveal to you every immoral past or present relationship in your life. Also, to self-reflect, ask yourself if you are constantly thinking about someone in a way that is obsessive or unhealthy? Do you feel emotionally or spiritually trapped in a relationship? Is there a connection that keeps you from moving forward with God?

As the Lord reveals them to you, repent and renounce the sin that opened the door, forgive the person, and sever the tie you have with the person in Jesus' Name. Ask the Lord to restore your soul and the soul of that person. As you go forward, remove any physical items that carry emotional or spiritual sentiments like letters, gifts, and photos. Keeping those items can reinforce the bond. Remove them as an act of faith and remain steadfast to guard yourself from ungodly relationships.

ABUSE AND TRAUMA

You may be thinking, how can abuse and trauma open the door to the enemy—especially when the victim did nothing to deserve such pain. The reality is that the devil preys on moments of vulnerability. Abuse, though never the fault of the victim, creates an opening for the enemy to gain access through the sin of the abuser and then the devil takes advantage of the emotional and spiritual pain experienced by the victim.

This is why soul healing is so important. When the devil gets in through a person's trauma, one of his goals is to cause the person to develop dysfunctional or maladaptive responses. It may come in the form of them trying to protect themselves by hiding, isolating, or emotionally shutting down. They may avoid people, resist connections, have a fragmented personality, or numb themselves with substances to avoid the pain. Regardless of the method the process to healing is blocked. This position is exactly where the devil wants to keep the person. The good news is that there is healing through Christ Jesus. Psalm 23:3 NKJV says it plainly "He restores my soul". The moment we give our trauma to Jesus is the moment the enemy loses his grip. We don't have to stay stuck in survival mode or be imprisoned by our pain. We can give our trauma to the Lord and He will restore us and make us whole.

SORORITIES & FRATERNITIES

Many people join organizations like sororities and fraternities to contribute to a greater cause, helping the community, feeding the hungry, or supporting children. These acts of charity and good deeds in and of themselves are not the problem. However, the issue arises when the rituals and initiations that are often required to join such groups are inserted. Some initiations involve public humiliation, shameful acts, or pledges of loyalty that are deeply symbolic and rooted in occult practices and Freemasonry. These rituals and oaths are far more than simple formalities; they are spiritual vows. When you swear an oath or pledge a vow of allegiance, knowingly or unknowingly, you are aligning yourself with everything that the oath represents, including any associated symbols, beliefs, or origins.

To have a clearer understanding of what this entails, some rituals may involve invoking spirits, participating in symbolic deaths and rebirths, or idol-like devotion to the organization. Greek life can subtly become an idol, taking the place in your heart that belongs to God. Loyalty to the organization, its rules, and its image can overshadow loyalty to Christ. People may also compromise their values to fit in or maintain their positions.

There are also testimonies online that you can search. Some believers have reported spiritual heaviness, confusion, emotional bondage, or attacks after pledging or joining Greek organizations, especially those with roots in occult practices or pagan symbols. Others have had to go through deliverance after renouncing their affiliation.

Again, people join fraternities or sororities with positive motives to help others, connect with like-minded people, and network. More often than not, they are unaware of the spiritual aspects hidden in the rituals, oaths, and vows. If you're already involved in a sorority or a fraternity, ask the Lord if what you are involved in is in alignment with Him. He will show you. Ask for wisdom, He will give it. Whatever is revealed to you, thank the Lord for showing it to you and then repent and renounce all organizations that are not in alignment with Him.

WORD CURSES

Proverbs 18:21 KJV delivers a powerful reminder: *"Death and life are in the power of the tongue: And they that love it shall eat the fruit thereof."* This proverb is a spiritual law. The words we speak are not empty sounds; they are seeds with the potential to grow into something life-giving or destructive. Every time we open our mouths, we run the risk of planting either a blessing or a curse, hope or despair, truth or deception—in our own lives and in the lives of others.

Think about how often we hear celebrities, artists, or people in the community at large say things like, "I won't live past 30," or "I'll never be happy." Tragically, many of those statements become self-fulfilling prophecies. But this isn't only about physical death—it's also about the death of dreams, the death of peace, or the withering of someone's confidence and calling. Our words carry weight. Phrases like "I always fail" or "I'll never change" may seem small, but they can slowly build invisible chains around a person's future.

We were made in the image and likeness of God, and as we read in Proverbs, our words matter. Just as God spoke the universe into existence with a simple "Let there be," According to Proverbs 18:21, we were created and designed with the ability to impact our lives with the words we release. Romans 12:14 NKJV helps us to have clarity, it says *"Bless and do not curse."* This is a call to actively choose life in our language—to bless people and situations instead of speaking out of frustration, bitterness, or fear. Blessing speaks to the potential in someone; cursing cuts it down. And every day, we are doing one or the other, whether we realize it or not.

Conversely, we must be aware that the enemy—the devil—cannot create. He doesn't have the ability to breathe life into anything. His strategy is to hijack our words. He tempts us to use our words destructively—to speak of death, division, doubt, and despair. Matthew 12:36 lets us know that we will give an account of every idle word. These are words that are unproductive, careless, void of purpose and value. We want to be sure that we are wise with our words and that we speak truth in love.

It is important to note that there is a stark difference between words spoken according to Proverbs 18:21 and the New Age concept of "name it and claim it". The power of our tongue is God-given and the words I am referencing are directly from our hearts (Luke 6:45). This is different from words from wishful thinking to manipulate and devise our own way. Words spoken from our hearts have consequences. We are to honor God and reflect moral responsibility with our speech. We are to have His Word (e.g scriptures) in our hearts to speak and declare out over our lives so that are lives line up with His spoken Word and promises. In contrast, the New Age concept of speaking into existence says that power is inherently controlled by the individual. In other words, the individual has the power to manipulate reality for personal empowerment, desires, and their own self will, never needing or submitting to the will of God.

CURSED OBJECTS

Cursed items are objects believed to carry negative spiritual influence or demonic power that can bring harm, misfortune, or negative consequences to those who possess them. In many cultures, certain objects can be seen as cursed if they are associated with evil spirits, idols, or sinful practices. From a biblical perspective, cursed items are often those that are linked to idolatry, occult practices, or sinful behavior.

Examples of cursed items can include:

1. Idols or Statues: Objects representing false gods or spirits. Often, they can be seen or presented as home decor and jewelry.

2. Occult Items: Tarot cards, Ouija boards, crystals, sage, and other items used for divination or contacting spirits.

3. Books or Artifacts Related to the Occult: Books on witchcraft, magic, or anything that promotes occult practices, such as spellbooks or materials related to Satanism, can carry spiritual contamination.

4. Objects Used in Sinful Practices: Items connected with sinful behaviors, such as pornographic material or items related to addictions (drugs, alcohol, gambling), can be seen as cursed due to their potential to lead people further away from God.

5. Gifts or Inherited Items from Occult Practices: If someone inherits or receives items from someone involved in the occult or witchcraft, those items could potentially carry spiritual consequences.

FINAL WORDS

This is only a brief list of potential ways the enemy can gain access or obtain legal ground to negatively influence our lives. The key is to be sensitive to the Holy Spirit and obedient to repent and renounce whatever

He reveals. If you are unsure, the Lord will not ignore your questions. He wants to reveal what is hurting you so you can be free and regain what has been lost. Prayer, accountability, and a life of obedience to God are key to guarding against these openings. By God's Grace and the leading of the Holy Spirit we can ensure that the devil does not have a foothold in our lives so that we remain under the Lord's protection.

SELF-REFLECTION QUESTIONS

1. Have I allowed anything into my life—through thoughts, words, or habits—that might be giving the enemy legal access or an open door into my life?

2. What is the Holy Spirit prompting me to surrender or change so that I can walk in freedom and protection under God's covering?

CHAPTER 11:
YOGA

Yoga has been around for centuries, yet many people are unaware of its true origins. Dating back thousands of years, yoga was created in India by a Hindu priest. While many people think of the poses as simple stretches or exercises, they are expressions of worship to various Hindu gods, and the mantras are considered prayers. What we see in Western society today is a modernized version presented as a physical workout, but the underlying purpose of the poses remains unchanged.

The word "yoga" means "to yoke," essentially meaning to unite or connect. But what many people don't realize is that this union was not about stretching, breathing, or inner calmness. According to those that understand and give testimony about it share that at its core, yoga was created as a spiritual practice designed to connect the individual to a spiritual being. This being is called Brahman, which is believed to represent ultimate reality. It is an impersonal life force that you "yoke" yourself with. Every yoga posture is "dedicated" to a specific Hindu deity for the purpose of invoking that deity to influence your life with manifestations and impartations for you to obtain their characteristics.

The Om Mantra chant that is repeated over and over again is an invocation of the three primary gods in Hinduism. Brahman the creator god, Vishnu the preserver god, and Shiva the destroyer god. So this mantra is asking these gods to manifest themselves in the person's body and spirit. The overall goal of yoga is to awaken the Kundalini spirit. Kundalini means serpent power. This power is believed to be a divine essence, a latent energy at the base of the spine that is coiled like a snake. Chanting the mantras, doing the breathing exercises, and performing the poses is for the purpose of awakening the serpent. When the serpent is "awakened", it can travel up the spine to various "chakra" levels for the purpose of achieving the chakra crown. The goal is to be spiritually awaken with a god consciousness and become one with the god invoked.

Let's be clear: the spiritual realm is real. All over the world, people are looking for "spiritual experiences." The question is not *whether* these experiences exist, but *what is the source*? Any spiritual connection that is not rooted in the one true God opens the door to deception—and ultimately to demonic influence.

In recent years, many former yoga instructors and practitioners have begun to speak out. At first, they saw yoga as harmless or even healing, but as they progressed deeper into practice, they began to experience dark spiritual manifestations, back pain, anxiety, nightmares, or unexplained heaviness. That's when the truth started to unfold—realizing they had unknowingly yoked themselves to spirits that were not from God.

These testimonies are now flooding social media as a warning to shed light on something that's often overlooked. The outward appearance of yoga may seem calm and positive, but spiritually, it can be a gateway that opens people up to things they never intended to invite in. The bottom line—we must be spiritually discerning. Ask yourself: *What am I aligning with? Who am I yoking myself to?* Because in the realm of the spirit, there's no such thing as neutrality. We're either connected to God or to something that's trying to pull us away from Him.

WHAT I LEARNED ABOUT YOGA

I first learned the truth about yoga in 1986, shortly after I became a Christian. I attended a Bible study at church, and during one of the sessions, we had a guest speaker who discussed yoga. Keep in mind that in 1986, yoga wasn't widely known the way it is today. It was my first time hearing about it. The speaker shared his concerns with urgency, warning us about what was coming and revealing the hidden dangers of yoga. He showed us videos of people who had been deeply involved in it, now warning others to stay away. These individuals spoke about how their lives were turned upside down by evil spirits, and for some, the negative consequences lingered long after they stopped practicing it.

To understand how I processed all this, it's important to consider the cultural context of 1986. Exercise in America at the time was dominated by aerobics and dance workouts—think "Flashdance"—spandex and leg warmers. I couldn't fathom why anyone would take yoga seriously, let alone embrace it as a legitimate form of exercise. Plus, considering it was presented as a religion in the videos, I couldn't see how it could ever be marketed as just another fitness trend.

I honestly didn't think yoga would catch on in the U.S. But over time, I watched it spread rapidly. Now, yoga classes are offered at nearly every gym or fitness studio, and the poses are often integrated into other workout routines for warm-ups and cool-downs. I've even heard of yoga being included in elementary school classrooms. Now I understand why the guest speaker had such an urgent message for us in 1986—he knew what was coming, and he wanted to make sure we knew the truth.

In 2004, I attended a hospital conference for continuing education credits, and one of the sessions on the agenda was yoga. Mid-morning, the yoga instructor came in with a warm smile and welcomed everyone. His demeanor was

kind and approachable, but I had no intention of participating. He instructed the group to close their eyes, clear
their minds, and repeat the sound "om."

As previously mentioned, in Hinduism, "om" represents the trinity of the three major gods: Brahma
(the creator), Vishnu (the preserver), and Shiva (the
destroyer). In the West, it's often presented as a way to
connect with your "higher self" or the universe, promoting deep meditation. Regardless, at its core, it's a
spiritual practice that uses the physical body to align
itself with various gods, connecting the participant with
demonic spirits.

As I looked around the room, I was struck by how
quickly everyone fell into the routine without questioning it. They didn't find the chanting of mantras or
humming the "om" strange. They closed their eyes and
participated willingly, not realizing the spiritual danger
they were engaging in.

Today, in addition to exercise, yoga is marketed as
a tool for relaxation, inner peace, and connecting with
your "inner light." It's often paired with meditation
practices that encourage people to empty their minds.
At first glance, emptying the mind may seem like a way
to achieve relaxation. However, it's a deliberate act of
surrendering control over your thoughts.

As Christians, we are never instructed to empty our
minds in meditation. Instead, we are called to meditate
on the Word of God day and night (Joshua 1:8). To

meditate on the Word of God means to deeply reflect, focus, and dwell on Scripture to understand it, apply it, and allow it to transform our hearts and minds. It's not just reading quickly or casually—it's an intentional, thoughtful engagement with God's truth.

The word *"meditate"* means "to mutter" or "to speak under one's breath." So meditating often includes speaking the Word aloud to yourself, repeating it, speaking and saying what God says in reference to your circumstances and situations and who you are. It strengthens faith and pushes back doubt. Meditating on Scripture is also about communion with God. It's not a mind-emptying experience like worldly meditation, but a heart-filling experience where you allow the Holy Spirit to bring revelation, conviction, comfort, and direction.

The ultimate goal of meditation is transformation. As the written words of the Bible take root, they begin to shape how we think, speak, and live. We begin to align with God's thoughts and reject lies from the enemy. Meditation leads to renewed thinking (Romans 12:2), deeper intimacy with God, and spiritual growth.

Overall, the physical movements and contortions of yoga are not exercise. There are countless ways to achieve physical health through traditional forms of movement. Engaging in yoga with its spiritual components contradict biblical teachings. As believers, we are encouraged to seek peace, healing, and relaxation through prayer, biblical meditation, and other activities that honor God.

We are not called to engage in practices with spiritual roots that draw us away from Him.

SELF-REFLECTION QUESTIONS

1. Am I engaging in spiritual practices of physical wellness that conflict with God's truth or open the door to spiritual compromise?

2. Have I asked the Holy Spirit to guide my choices in areas like exercise or meditation, to ensure that they align with God's Word and honor Him fully?

CHAPTER 12:
HOW I KNOW HELL IS REAL

There are countless testimonies from people who have had near-death experiences (NDEs), and many of them speak with unshakable conviction about what they saw. Whether it was a glimpse of heaven or a terrifying encounter with hell, these stories are truly sobering. Simultaneously, it is also beautiful to see them turn their lives around and share their compelling experiences with others and lead them to Christ.

You may be familiar with popular accounts like *A Divine Revelation of Hell* and *A Divine Revelation of Heaven* by Mary Kay Baxter or Bill Wiese's book, *23 Minutes in Hell.* These testimonies have touched countless lives, and to me, they're a clear testament of how deeply the Lord loves us, as He does not want anyone to perish and spend eternity in hell (2 Peter 3:9).

In chapter seven, I shared some key insights about spiritual warfare—specifically, how the mind is primarily where our battles take place. It was during that same season of learning and growing that I had a personal experience I want to share with you. At that time, I had not learned the depth of Proverbs 23:7 yet. Instead, the Lord was opening my eyes to understand something else.

As I stated in chapter seven, I did not understand spiritual warfare, nor did I understand the fear, anxiety and insomnia I was experiencing. It was so intense that I simply wanted God to step in and make it go away. After struggling with it for some time, I grew frustrated, wondering why I couldn't shake the fear that plagued me. I was struggling with my faith, questioning everything every time the enemy threw lies at me. At my lowest, I thought, *maybe a trip to hell would wake me up and straighten me out.* I know it sounds crazy, but I asked for such and experience. Let me just say, I am thankful that in God's infinite love and mercy He knew my request was misguided and He did not grant me that request. But He did allow me to have a glimpse of something that I'll never forget.

For a long time, I kept this experience to myself, only sharing it with family and a few close friends. I was embarrassed to talk about it openly, fearing that people would think I was crazy or that it wasn't real. But over time, I realized I couldn't keep it hidden. It wasn't my job to make others believe; it was simply my responsibility to share what happened.

As I stated earlier, I was struggling with insomnia. There were days when I barely slept at all, despite working full-time and raising children. Sometimes, I went nights without any sleep. Those rare occasions when I did manage to get a few hours of rest, it was never more than about two or three hours. I became so desperate for sleep that I longed for nothing more than to wake up rested, hearing the birds chirping in the morning.

One night, when I did manage to fall asleep, I woke up abruptly, as if there was a strange noise in the night. No stretching or yawning, just a sudden, full awareness. Then, I experienced something that is hard to explain. As I opened my eyes, I felt something deep within me trembling. It was my internal organs trembling like a skeleton being shaken on a string or a person's teeth chattering from the cold. I had never experienced anything like that before. The cause was fear. Not just any fear, but more like terror, pure and raw—It was tangible. No horror movie could compare to the kind of fear I was feeling. Along with that fear, there was an overwhelming sense of hopelessness, like a never-ending dread that would never, ever change.

From the moment I opened my eyes and was overwhelmed with terror and hopelessness, I thought instantly: *This must be what hell feels like.* I can't explain how or why that thought came to me, but I knew that it was an accurate description of what I was experiencing. Somehow, amid all that fear and hopelessness with my internal organs shaking, I managed to sit up on the side of my bed. I immediately began to pray whatever words came to mind. I don't remember what I said exactly. All I know is that I called out to Jesus. And in that instant, everything I felt, every ounce of terror and all the hopelessness lifted. The atmosphere returned to normal. I didn't know what to think; all I wanted to do was thank the Lord over and over again.

Over the next few days after that brief yet profound experience, a few things stood out to me. First, the terror I felt was something I couldn't imagine enduring for all eternity. For the first time, I understood how those who have experienced an NDE struggled to formulate a description of what that terror feels like. It's not just an emotional fear, but a physical terror that caused me to tremble on the inside, something I could never recreate or demonstrate.

The second thing that struck me was the hopelessness. Here on earth, we can find hope in so many things. We have the opportunity to see the sun rise every morning. We can look forward to a new day or a smile from a friend. Picnics, vacations, graduations, or just a simple day to relax and do nothing. However, this hopelessness was unlike anything I've ever known. And what made it so horrific was that the hopelessness was a reflection of the absolute absence of God. Whether we realize it or not, the Spirit of God is present and active on earth. But Hell is truly a place where people are separated from Him. Instead of love, there is hate. Instead of light, there is darkness. Instead of hope, there is hopelessness. Hell is the opposite of everything good. And when you add the hellfire, torment, and demons (which, thank God, I did not experience), I can't comprehend encountering that on top of everything else I experienced in those moments.

Another profound realization was that I had the opportunity to call on Jesus. People in hell don't have that chance. That thought hit me deeply. In my moment of despair, I could call on His name, and He responded immediately. That simple act of calling on Him was enough to rescue me. Romans 10:13 NKJV says, *For "whoever calls on the name of the LORD shall be saved."* And Joel 2:32 KJV says, *"And it shall come to pass, that whoever calls on the name of the LORD shall be delivered:…".* I experienced the power of calling on His name firsthand. Here on earth, it's that simple—when we call on the name of the Lord, He responds.

You may be wondering, what does this experience have to do with spiritual warfare and deliverance? I think this experience and countless others shows us God's desire to save. Through them we can see our need for salvation, healing, deliverance, and our total dependence upon the Lord. Without these experiences and testimonies, we can easily get caught up in the day-to-day routine and forget that there truly is a war going on for our souls.

Hell is a real place that the Lord saved us from, and He wants us to share that truth with others. Hell was never meant for us. When Satan rebelled against God and wanted to rule "his" own kingdom, the Lord allowed him to have what he wanted. A dark kingdom void and opposite of the things of God. Hell was prepared for Satan and his fallen angels, not for mankind (Matthew 25: 41b). Satan chose darkness over light, torment over peace, hopelessness over hope. And now, he's desperate to take as many people as he can with him.

When Satan looks at us, he sees the image of God, and he hates it. He hates that we were made in God's image and likeness. Satan tries to do whatever he can to make us look more like him and less like Jesus. It all started in the Garden of Eden, when Satan tempted Adam and Eve to sin. Their choice to eat from the forbidden tree introduced sin into the world, and since then, sin has separated mankind from God. If we remain in sin, we will end up in the same place that was prepared for Satan, which is *permanent* separation from God for all eternity.

But God, in His infinite wisdom and love, didn't leave us with no way out. Jesus came, lived a perfect life without sin, and then died for our sins. He became the sinless sacrifice, shedding His blood to wash our sins away. He demonstrated that He has all power and authority over death, hell, and the grave when He rose again.

This is the Gospel Satan doesn't want anyone to hear. He wants to keep people from repenting, believing in Jesus, and from calling on His name. He wants us to think we can be good enough on our own or that we can sin without consequences. But the truth is, hell is real. It's a place of hopelessness, torment, and eternal separation from God.

The devil is running out of time, and he knows it. He knows he lost, but he's still trying to deceive as many as he can. Those fallen angels are forever regretful for following him. I don't want that to be anyone's future.

If you don't know Jesus, I encourage you to invite Him into your heart today. You don't need to get yourself together first. As a Christian, back then, I thought I needed to, but all I needed to do was call on His name. Jesus wants you to come as you are. We can't fix ourselves, but His grace transforms us. We come as we are, but by His Spirit, we don't stay as we are.

He loves you so much that He left His throne in heaven to take on human flesh, perform miracles, cast out demons, and ultimately die for our sins. A Holy and Just God can't coexist with sin, but He didn't discard us. He made a way for us to be saved through the cross. Jesus took the sins of the entire world upon Himself so that anyone who chooses Him can be saved.

Pray this simple prayer with me today:

Dear Jesus,

I believe that You are the Son of God and that You died for my sins. Your Word says in the Bible that if I come to You, You will not cast me out (John 6:37). As I come, I ask that You forgive me and wash away all my sins. Thank You Lord. Your Word also says that if I confess with my mouth "Lord Jesus," and believe in my heart that God raised You from the dead, I will be saved (Romans 10:9-10). Lord, I believe. I renounce the kingdom of darkness, and I confess You as Lord, and I thank You that salvation has been granted to me. I ask that You come into my heart today and show me by the Holy Spirit how to live and walk through this life journey. Thank You so much for forgiving me and demonstrating Your Perfect Love towards me.

Amen

SECTION VI:
STAYING FREE –
BE FREE INDEED

WARFARE AND DELIVERANCE

TANYA D. NORWOOD

CHAPTER 13:
WALKING IN LIBERTY

In the Bible, we see that when someone is healed or delivered, Jesus often instructs them to *"go, and sin no more"* (John 8:11 KJV). Once we experience freedom, we are called to responsibly maintain it. I heard one minister say that deliverance gets the demons out, but living as the Lord's disciple *keeps* them out. This powerful statement highlights the fact that deliverance is just the beginning. To stay free, we must live intentionally disciplined lives, continually aligning ourselves with God's Word.

The word *"discipline"* shares its roots with the word *"disciple."* As Christians, we must understand that freedom isn't a passive state; it requires active, ongoing commitment. It's not enough to simply be delivered; we must cultivate habits that keep us free. We need to take the time to study and apply the principles of the Bible in our everyday lives. This includes renewing our minds to think as God instructs us and allowing our character to be shaped through humility and obedience. In addition to obedience, growth and transformation can take place through fasting, prayer, reading scripture, worship, and declaring God's Word over our lives. Intertwined with all of this, is just spending time with God. Being in His presence is transformative in itself.

As it relates to staying free, we have already discussed how Jesus warns in Matthew 12:43-45 that when a demon leaves a person, it will try to return with more demons, seeking to reclaim previous ground. This is not for us to live in constant worry about losing our freedom, but we do need to stay vigilant and mindful not to give the devil a foothold.

A few years ago, I heard a testimony from a believer that I think will help illustrate the concept of staying free. He experienced trauma after being sexually abused as a teen. Afterwards, as a Christian he struggled with a spirit of perversion, same-sex attraction, and pornography. Some years later, wanting to be free, he sought the Lord through eight days of fasting and prayer. He was delivered, however, later he found himself returning to secular television and movies, which, while not overtly pornographic, it still contained a lot of sexual content. By resuming the visual diet he had consumed prior to his deliverance, he soon realized that he had reopened the door to the spirits of lust and perversion that he had been previously freed from.

His experience serves as both a sobering warning and a vivid reminder of how quickly spiritual doors can be reopened, even after a season of genuine humility, prayer, and fasting. It wasn't that God had failed, instead he had given the enemy access again. Thankfully by resubmitting himself to the Lord and closing those doors through fasting and prayer, he experienced deliverance again. His testimony underscores the vital importance of guarding our hearts and minds from the things we allow in.

His testimony also underscores the vital role of fasting. Not only can fasting play a role in deliverance, but it also will help us break free from stubborn strongholds. As we consecrate our hearts we are positioned to hear the Lord. Fasting humbles us and with humility we can also see areas in our character that need to be transformed. This humility, coupled with our desire to be changed, positions us to stay free. It also protects us from returning to sinful habits or behaviors.

Another vital key to maintaining spiritual freedom is developing a healthy, reverential fear of the Lord. Proverbs 16:6b KJV tells us, *"And by the fear of the LORD men depart from evil."* While it's easy to center our walk with God around His love and grace, which are at the core of our salvation, it's just as important not to lose sight of His Holiness and the awe-inspiring power of His presence.

God's love draws us close, and His grace gives us the strength to change, but it's the fear of the Lord that keeps us grounded in obedience. It's not fear in the sense of being so terrified that you run away from Him, but a fear that draws you close with deep reverence, respect, and awareness of who God truly is. Acknowledging His majesty, His sovereignty, and His ability to both bless and correct. He is a Holy and Just God, perfectly balancing meekness and authority.

Take Abraham for example. In Genesis 22:12b NLT, when he was prepared to offer Isaac as a sacrifice, the angel of the LORD stopped him and said, *"...for now I know that you truly fear God. You have not withheld from me even your son, your only son."* God describe Abraham's radical obedience as a fear of Him. Yes Abraham believed God and he was fully persuaded that God would keep His promise. He believed that God would make him the father of many nations, even if he had to raise Isaac from the dead to do it. But what is highlighted in this scripture was Abraham's fear of the Lord.

The Bible also tells us in Proverbs 9:10 KJV that *"The fear of the LORD is the beginning of wisdom:"*. When we walk in that kind of Holy fear, we begin to make wise choices that reflect our reverence for God. This kind of wisdom helps us avoid sin, resist temptation, and discern what's truly good and pleasing in God's eyes. In short, the fear of the Lord doesn't push us away—it anchors us, it deepens our devotion, and it helps us to stay free.

Lastly, freedom is available in God's presence. When we spend time reading God's Word and when we sit still in His presence with prayer and worship no devil will want to sit and dwell in that atmosphere. By default things will fall off. You look up and realize that some of the things you were struggling with, you don't struggle with them anymore. When we abide and dwell in His presence, the only response that we can experience is transformative change.

SELF-REFLECTION QUESTIONS

1. Am I living my life as a disciple, where I allow Jesus to be Savior and Lord over every area of my life?

2. Is my life lived a reflection of the "fear of the Lord" or an unbalanced focus on hyper-grace?

CONCLUSION

WARFARE AND DELIVERANCE

TANYA D. NORWOOD

CHAPTER 14:
A FEW WORDS OF ENCOURAGEMENT

One of the things I love about the Lord is that, despite the challenges and battles we face, He always encourages us. One Word from God in the middle of a storm can bring peace and comfort, reminding us that everything is okay. That encouragement might come from the Bible, another person, a message, or a word directly from Him to our spirit. The Lord can use whatever method He chooses, but one way He speaks to us that I would like to share with you is found in Zephaniah 3:17 (NLT). It reads, *"The LORD your God is living among you. He is a mighty savior. He will take delight in you with gladness. With his love, he will calm all your fears. He will rejoice over you with joyful songs."*

This scripture is one that can stir our hearts deeply. First, it speaks to God's ever-present nature—He's not a distant unreachable God. He is *living* among us. This is not just a God who exists somewhere far away, but one who actively dwells with us in our everyday lives. We are temples of the Holy Spirit.

He is also described as a "mighty Savior." This emphasizes His power and ability to save us, not just in a distant, abstract way, but in real and tangible ways in our daily struggles.

Lastly, the second half of this verse truly takes us into something incredible. It says, "He will rejoice over you with joyful songs." This is one of those truths that's hard to fully grasp but is absolutely beautiful once we do. Imagine this: God, Elohim, the Mighty Creator of the entire universe—the One who spoke the stars into existence, who formed the mountains and the oceans, and who holds the entire world in His hands—chooses to take time out of His eternal existence to sing over YOU.

Consider how remarkable this is! Out of the billions of people on this planet, He's not too busy, too distant, or too removed to stop and sing with joy over *you.* Think about that for a moment. It's a personal and intimate act that reveals the depth of His love for you. He takes delight in you, not just as part of the world's population, but as an individual who He values deeply.

Many of you might already have experienced God's presence in this way, perhaps in moments when you felt overwhelmed or uncertain, and a song of peace or joy seemed to come from nowhere, filling your heart and reminding you of His love. But for those who may not have felt this, let me share two personal stories that illustrate this beautiful truth.

FOR NEW BELIEVERS

Often, new believers may question if they are truly saved. They look for a sign or a feeling of validation. Some time ago, I was questioning that very thing. Was I truly saved? Here is how the Lord encouraged me. One night, unable to sleep, I suddenly heard a soft voice in my spirit singing the lyrics to a song:

Blessed assurance,
Jesus is mine.
Oh, what a foretaste,
Of glory divine.
Heir of salvation,
Purchased of God.
Born of His Spirit,
Washed in His blood.
This is my story,
This is my song,
Praising my Savior,
All the day long.[1]

---

1   "Blessed Assurance." Blue Letter Bible. Accessed 13 May, 2025. https://www.blueletterbible.org/hymns/b/Blessed_Assurance.cfm

At first, I didn't fully understand what was going on. The song was playing softly within me. It wasn't a song I listened to often, and honestly I had not thought about it in a long time. As I began to pay attention to the lyrics, it clicked. *Blessed assurance.* The Lord was *speaking to me!* I am saved! As I listened and allowed those words to sink in, they were consoling. Hearing the words *"Heir of salvation", was so comforting. Salvation was "my" inheritance. A gift to me that was not* secured based on my own efforts, but because His Love purchased me, His Blood washed me, and His Spirit lives in me.

This song was written in 1873, but as I rehearsed the lyrics over and over in my mind, in those moments, it was as if that song was written just for me. I began to understand the title *Blessed Assurance* in a brand-new way.

Perhaps many of you have experienced a song rise within you, giving you encouragement and strength for the day. For me, I have learned to pay attention to songs that come into my heart unexpectedly. It's not necessarily something I heard recently, instead it's something that seems to rise up out of nowhere, right when my heart is heavy or my mind is occupied with concerns. In the midst of those moments, a melody starts playing quietly in the background of my thoughts. It may seem random at first, but when I pause and really pay attention, I begin to realize: *the song is speaking directly to what I am going through—bringing comfort, clarity, and reassurance.*

God knows every detail of our lives. If He chooses, He can use a song to speak. He knows how music can bypass our mental defenses and reach down to the deepest part of us. Through these moments, we are reminded that He sees us, He is with us, and He knows exactly what we need to hear. So when a song suddenly begins to echo in your heart in the middle of your busy day or during a quiet night, don't brush it off. Pause. Listen. Ask God, "Are You speaking to me through this?" You might just find that the melody is His way of wrapping you in His presence and reminding you that you are not alone.

FOR ALL BELIEVERS

Continuing in the theme of Zephaniah 3:17, the Lord knows how to really encourage us when we are doing everything we can to stand. We already know how the story ends—we win! But let's be honest, there are days when we don't necessarily feel like conquerors. Sometimes the battles can make us feel weary and the weight of it can make victory feel distant as if someone keeps moving the finish line. But God is always faithful to step in.

There was a day when I felt completely worn down—like every battle I was facing just wouldn't let up. It seemed like I was fighting on all sides with no rest in sight. One night in bed as I was trying to rest, I heard music. Not a song with lyrics, but an instrumental piece. I could hear a beautiful blend of rich orchestra sounds of horns, bassoons, clarinets, flutes, and oboes coming together—a symphony. Though no words were spoken, the music carried a message. What was incredible was that I recognized the melody. In hindsight I may have responded with "Really Lord, the Rocky song?"

It was the theme from the movie *Rocky*. In a short clip of the movie, the main character, Rocky Balboa, runs through the streets of the city (we are in a race). As he runs, all these children begin to run with him as they cheer him on (all God's children are in this race). As he continues to run, he begins to shadowbox periodically (we are fighting spiritual battles). Approaching the Philadelphia Museum, he sprints up the series of stairs (it's not always easy to climb, but God gives us strength). He then finishes the race at the top of the stairs at the Philadelphia Museum of Art, raising his hands in victory. He won! He endured until the very end (Matthew 24:13). With an instrumental piece, the Lord was encouraging me without using a single word! Yet the messaged screamed "VICTORY"!

To every believer reading this, don't give up. Your race does not go unnoticed. You are surrounded by a great cloud of witnesses, and God Himself is with you, strengthening you each step of the way.

And the Lord will deliver me from every evil work and preserve *me* for His heavenly kingdom. To Him *be* glory forever and ever. Amen!

–2 TIMOTHY 4:18 NKJV

www.ingramcontent.com/pod-product-compliance
Lightning Source LLC
Chambersburg PA
CBHW051315120626
46547CB00015B/2254

* 9 7 9 8 2 1 8 7 8 4 9 4 2 *